CRYPTOCURRENCIES IN THE INTERNATIONAL SCENARIO

iii

Dedicated to my father Carlos
Revoredo, for showing me the
importance of always keeping an
open mind.
To my mother, Maria Lucia, for
teaching me the wisdom of patience,
persistence and delicacy in achieving
the goals.

To Brie for her unconditional
dedication and make me believe in
the impossible.

And to my friend Rodrigo, for the
partnership, encouragement and
unyielding enthusiasm.

Dedicated to Renata, my love,
for all support, dedication and
patience. It wouldn´t be
possible without you by my
side.

To my family for always
supporting me and believing in
my dreams.

Special thanks to
my friend and
partner Tatiana,
for the
partnership.

v

Table of Contents

CHAPTER 2 |
CRYPTOCURRENCIES
ECOSYSTEM AND ITS
CHALLENGES.................................. 26

CHAPTER 3 | CENTRAL BANKS
REACTION TO THE
CRYPTOCURRENCIES 35

CHAPTER 1 | A BRIEF INTRODUCTION TO THE CRYPTO UNIVERSE

Introduction

The emergence of cryptocurrencies has allowed the emergence of a new class of "virtual assets" which, due to their constant economic and legal evolution, have aroused different interpretations, representing a great challenge for regulators all over the world (Revoredo, 2018).

Currently, there are over 1,911 cryptocurrencies in circulation (CoinMarketCap, 2018), but many of them are not considered cryptocurrencies in the terminological sense of the term[1]. Ether, for example, listed with ETH code and widely traded in brokerage firms, is an electronic token device used as "fuel" within the Ethereum platform to run smart contracts and computing services within the Internet (Revoredo, 2017).

Having this in mind, in this book, we will see if it is correct to classify Bitcoin as money, as well as a brief analysis of the evolution of cryptocurrencies among Countries.

Let's start with a brief introduction about the crypto universe.

The crisis of trust in the traditional model of centralized organizations and institutions

With the advent of digitalization of society and the Web Economy (Revoredo, 2017), despite online trade and electronic payments almost exclusively with the brokering of financial institutions, the demand for "digital money" has come up.

Here, we are not talking about electronic currency (which is a representation of fiat currency, issued by a Central Bank)[1] or the use of credit card in an online shop, but yet of that "digital asset" which brings reliability, privacy, transparency (of the transactions) and speed to operations on the Internet.

The uncountable scandals involving governments, financial institutions, and big corporations have motivated society to search for solutions for the

---

[1] The difference between electronic currency and cryptocurrency will be analyzed in detail later

numerous problems caused by the centralized pattern of data transfer and commercial transactions. For those who wish to understand this crisis of trust better, I suggest watching the US documentary, "Dirty Money" that shows corruption schemes in the US corporations.

In the last twenty years, economy progressively backed out from the traditional model of centralized organizations and institutions where big operators, many times with a dominant position, were responsible for rendering services to a group of passive consumers (De Filippi, 2017).

As far as the participation of intermediates for granting transactions between individuals refrained from fulfilling the needs of a globalized and interconnected world, it was a matter of time until human intelligence could design a solution for satisfying the new social ambitions.

In this scenario is that the first cryptocurrency (Bitcoin) and the architecture (Blockchain) that allows its operation arose.

Let's find out how this happened.

Blockchain Bitcoin as a disruptive structure [2]

The cryptocurrency, assets of the gender digital currency, is a virtual monetary tool that uses cryptography to secure transactions and control the creation of new units of the currency. The most famous of them is bitcoin, created in 2009 by Satoshi Nakamoto.

Bitcoin allows you to make financial transactions without a broker, verified by "us" (the network participants) P2P (Peer-to-Peer) and recorded in a distributed architecture called Blockchain.

Thus, the Blockchain Bitcoin architecture allows such data to be transmitted to all the participants of the network, in a decentralized and transparent way, making unnecessary the work of a broker to guarantee the accounting and reliability of the relations developed through the Internet.

This way, the network will contain the history of every transaction and cryptographic ownership of all bitcoins from the creator's address up to the current

---

[2] This topic was the subject of an article published on October 5,2017. Revoredo, Tatiana. In: *"Which problems have Cryptocurrencies come to solve? Blockchain Bitcoin as a disruptive technology."* Medium, 2017.

address. The information registered in this ledger (blockchain) is unchangeable so that in case a user tries to reuse "coins" which have already been used ("double use"), the whole network of computers taking part of the Bitcoin Blockchain, which is decentralized, will reject the transaction.

With the decentralization of the Bitcoin network and the absence of a central administrator, it is impossible for any governmental entity to manipulate the emission and the value of the bitcoins or even to induce inflation by "printing" new coins.

Besides the evident advantages of the decentralization of the Bitcoin network, which problems has Bitcoin come to solve?

Now, much more than software running on computers spread around the world, it is a network of independent electronic transfers of a third part, which enliven a free monetary system through the Internet. Its invention, however, came to unravel something much bigger: the problems inherent in the current centralized system of financial transfer and intermediation. Let us check the main ones (Centralized Monetary Policy, intermediation costs, privacy, safety, and double spending).

Bitcoin, with its controlled and limited emission, through software, simulating the commodities extraction rate like gold and silver, comes to oppose the centralized Monetary Policy. The reason is that the fusion of banks and State gives the opportunity for eventual manipulation and use of the financial system focusing on regulating "market overflow" and "stimulating economy." To the detriment of the purchasing power of the whole population, eventually, decisions may be taken to benefit a minority strategically positioned in the political environment.

Moreover, the cryptocurrency comes to solve the problem of the intermediation costs. Trade on the Internet uses financial institutions as intermediate for payment processing, what makes the value of transactions way too expensive, impairing the borderless business of the Internet.

On the other hand, Bitcoin arises as a warrantor of people's privacy, opposing itself against the current financial system, which demands a series of personal information to put a transaction in place. At the Bitcoin network, each person owns only one or more pairs of 'keys" used to attribute ownership of an amount of bitcoins—none of this linked to an identity. Here, the cryptocurrency technically jibes with physical cash: there is no need to the seller know the buyer nor the origin of their money[3].

---

[3] Tax Policy and Anti-Money Laundry (AML) will be addressed in the next chapter

Furthermore, in possession of so much information, the banks naturally become excellent targets to cybernetic attacks and cons, in a way that our information is at the mercy of the employer's honesty and of the safety of their systems. In a decentralized network, this lack of Safety does not exist. It is transferred to the user, though, the responsibility of adopting proper protection methods to their access keys.

Finally, Bitcoin solves the malfunctioning of Double Spending, (or the canceling of payment after the receipt of a product or service), once, given its decentralized nature, even currently taking around ten minutes for having more reliability, the bitcoin transaction becomes irreversible.

Here it is the disruptive character of the cryptocurrency, which has taken market capitalization to a significant advancement, with the current value superior to US$ 146 million (according to a query made on 09/01/2018 at the website coinmarketcap.com).

What is decentralization?[4]

Decentralization removes the need for powerful central authorities

One of the most exciting aspects of Blockchain architecture is that it is entirely decentralized, rather than stored in one central point. This removes the need for powerful central authorities and instead hands control back to the individual user. But how does this system work? What does it mean for our future ?

Why is it so revolutionary?

The decentralized nature of blockchain architecture means that it doesn't rely on a central point of control. A lack of a single authority makes the system fairer and considerably more secure. The way in which data is recorded onto a blockchain epitomizes one of its most revolutionary quality: its value of decentralization. Rather than relying on a central authority to securely transact with other users, blockchain utilizes consensus protocols to validate

---

[4] Lisk Academy. In: Benefits of blockchain: what is decentralization, Lisk, 2018

transactions and record data in a manner that is incorruptible.

As the system does not rely on a central authority, the fees that are normally collected by these organisations are no longer a factor. Therefore, transacting on the blockchain are cheaper, as the only costs incurred by the parties involved are the nominal fees used to reward the miner or forgers that run a node on the network.

Furthermore, the information recorded on the blockchain can be certain to be true as it is near impossible to manipulate due to there being multiple copies that require a complex consensus to be edited. On top of that in combination with the role played by cryptographic hash functions in the system.

The data is made even more secure by the fact that there is no reliance on a central point of storage, reducing the risk of it being lost or destroyed. Attacking one point of storage would result in no loss of data since all the information is stored on multiple devices around the world. In this regard Bitcoin is the most weathered and resilient platform in the space, having withstood barrages of attempted hacks, all of which have been unsuccessful.

Decentralization vs. Cloud Storage

Decentralization is not to be confused with traditional cloud storage. Data that is stored in the cloud is not stored directly on a device but still kept on one central server elsewhere. Unlike blockchain, this is still very much a centralized solution.

> Data that is stored on the blockchain is not stored on a single device, but rather distributed across many different devices across a P2P network (peer-to-peer network).

What is Peer to Peer Network?

A Peer to Peer (abbreviated to P2P) network is a very important part of how Blockchain works, and why it is so solid and secure.

> A peer-to-peer network is one in which two or more computers share files and access to devices without requiring a separate server computer or server software.

10

Peer-to-peer (P2P) networking is a distributed application architecture that shares tasks or workloads between peers. Peers are equally privileged, equipotent participants in the application. They are said to form a peer-to-peer network of nodes.

What is a Consensus Protocol?

A consensus protocol is a set of rules that describe how the communication and transmission of data between electronic devices, such as nodes, works.

> Consensus is achieved when enough devices are in agreement about what is true andwhat should be recorded onto a blockchain.

Therefore, consensus protocols are the governing rules that allow devices that are scattered across the world to factually come to an agreement, allowing a blockchain network to function without being corrupted.[5]

---

[5] Idem Reference 4

A comparative analysis between money, currency, digital money, fiat money, electronic money and cryptocurrencies.

What's money? What's currency?

Money is, in its most basic form, any method to transfer some type of value from on person to the next. Food, salt, animal hides, gold, silver, each has already been serverd as money at one time or another. [6]

> A currency is the actual execution of the theoretical concept of money.

Currencies under economic perspective

At first, it is important to notice that economists consider something as currency when it encompasses

---

[6] Hosp, Dr. Julian. In: Cryptocurrencies: Bitcoin, Ethereum, Blockchain, ICO's & Co. simply Explained, 2017.

the following three features: medium of exchange, unit of account and stock of value.

Especially in countries where government credibility is in free decay, as it is the case of Venezuela, we can realize that more and more people are willing to keep Bitcoin to protect themselves from an economic crisis and the harming effects of inflation (stock of value.)[7]

Notwithstanding, although more and more retailers do accept crypto coins as a method of payment (medium of exchange), under economic perspective, Bitcoin can't be considered a currency "yet," once the high volatility has discouraged its use for pricing of products and services (unit of account.)

Here, it is essential to highlight the notes made by Monica de Bolle[8] regarding what a coin is.

> Before paper money, before currency-liability which value depends on the confidence in the government that creates and destroys it, a coin was a good, an asset, like the gold coins that

---

[7] Revoredo, Tatiana. In: *Criptomoedas: cenário global e tendências*, Jota, on October 27, 2017

[8] Economist and researcher at the Peterson Institute for International Economics and Professor at Sais/Johns Hopkins University

held value, not because they were golden and shiny, but because they were precious metals. And such currency-goods or asset-coins comply with the same functions of the paper money (they are used for quoting prices, they are used as a means of exchange, saved to stock value).

However, they do not depend on the solidity of any government, for they have intrinsic value, something that paper money does not have.

It is in this latter sense that the cryptocurrencies, attacked today by economists worldwide, not incidentally are called digital gold.[9]

Cryptocurrencies have intrinsic value.

Intrinsic value that is in the operational systems, in the Blockchain structures, without which these virtual assets would not exist.

---

[9] Bölle, M. d., In: *O que é moeda? O Estado de São Paulo*, on February 7, 2018

Thus, while cryptocurrencies still do not satisfactorily comply with the functions of a currency as described above, it is a fact that cryptocurrencies are with us since the advent of Bitcoin, soon after the crisis of 2008. Almost ten years later not only the term "bitcoin" has become well known in general, but several other crypto coins came up from technological platforms more or less alike to those created by Satoshi Nakamoto.[10]

Currencies from a legal perspective

Now, from a legal aspect, for crypto coins like Litecoin and TeslaColilCoin be coins, legal tender is required. Let us elaborate on it:

From a legal viewpoint, cryptocurrencies are "currency" if the law so defines.[11]

---

[10] Idem Reference 8

[11] Revoredo, T. In: Criptomoedas: analise comparativa com moeda eletrônica e moeda estrangeira, Criptomoedas Fácil, on August 27, 2018

As an example, we can mention Germany that promoted Bitcoin to the category of legal tender and, therefore, equivalent to currency from the legal point of view, when used as a means of payment.[12]

Now, in countries whose law does not confer it such quality, like in Brazil, Bitcoin positions itself int the opposite direction of **fiduciary currencies** (those whose value comes from the trust that people have in those who issued them). In those countries, there are those who consider Bitcoin as a foreign currency.

That is what currencies are from the legal and economic point of view.

Cryptocurrencies vs. electronic money

Electronic Coins are resources stored in an electronic device or system that allows the end user to carry out a payment transaction in national currency.

Cryptocurrencies have their own form, that is, they are distinct units of account of currencies issued by sovereign governments, and there are no electronic device or system for storage in fiat money.

---

[12] Bundesministerium der Finanzen. In: Umsatzsteuerliche behandlung von bitcoin und anderen sog virtuellen waehrungen, on February 27, 2018.

Cryptocurrencies are a kind of digital currency, not to be confused with electronic money.

Electronic money are issued by the state and made available in digital format.[13]

Cryptocurrencies vs. digital currencies

Digital money are money used on the internet.

"Digital money exists only in the digital form. It doesn't have any physical equivalent in the real world. Nevertheless, it has all the characteristics of traditional money. Just as classic fiat money, you can obtain, transfer or exchange it for another currency. You can use it to pay for the goods and services, such as mobile and Internet communication, online stores and others. Digital currencies don't have geographical or political borders; transactions might be

---

[13] Revoredo, T. In Blockchain we trust: conheça o novo guardião da confiança. Criptomoedas Fácil, July 26, 2018

> sent from any place and received an any point in the world."[14]

With less than ten years of existence, crypto-coins are such a new asset that conceptualizing them becomes a Herculean activity[15].

> "The costly task of defining what cryptocurrencies are derives mainly from two factors:
>
> 1) The difficulty of qualifying its essence
>
> 2) the impossibility of tracking the size of the impact of something still under development."

Though **cryptocurrency is a type of digital currency**, there are some fundamental differences.

> Digital currencies are centralized; there is a group of people and computers that regulates the state of the transactions in the network. Cryptocurrencies are decentralized,

---

[14] Tar, Andrew. In: *Digital Currencies vs. Cryptocurrencies, Explained.* Cointelegraph. December 13, 2017.

[15] Idem Reference 11

and the regulations are made by the majority of the community. Digital currencies require user identification. You'll need to upload a photo of yourself and some documents issued by the public authorities. Buying, investing and any other processes with cryptocurrencies do not need require any of that. Nevertheless, cryptocurrencies are not fully anonymous. Though the addresses don't contain any confidential information such as name, residential address, etc., each transaction is registered, the senders and the receivers are publicly known. Thus, all the transactions are tracked[16].

There are even companies that perform this tracking, and help prevent, detect and investigate cryptocurrencies money laundering, fraud and compliance violations like Chainalysis[17] and Elliptic[18].

---

[16] Tar, Andrew. In: Digital Money vs. Cryptocurrencies, Explained. Cointelegraph, on December 13, 2017.

[17] Chainalysis is a compliance and research software for the world's top institutions. Its Blockchain Intelligence Platform is able to cryptocurrency transaction monitoring in real-

"Digital currencies are not transparent. You cannot choose the address of the wallet and see all the money transfers. This information is confidential. Cryptocurrencies are transparent. Everyone can see any transactions of any user, since all the revenue streams are placed in a public chain.

Digital currencies have a central authority that deals with issues. It can cancel or freeze transactions upon the request of the participant or authorities or on suspicion of fraud or money-laundering. Cryptocurrencies are regulated by the community. It's very unlikely that the users will approve the changes in the Blockchain,

---

time with raises real-time alerts on incoming and outgoing transactions for links to potentially suspicious activity. Its compliance analysts get dynamically updated customer risk profiles with the most up to date information from the blockchain for periodic reviews. Also, Chainalysis uses pattern recognition, machine learning and millions of open source references to identify and categorize 1,000's of cryptocurrency services.

[18] Elliptic identify illicit activity in cryptocurrencies, providing actionable intelligence to cryptocurrency companies, financial institutions and government agencies.

although there were some precedents such as the hack of The DAO." [19] [20]

---

[19] Tar, Andrew. In: Digital Money vs. Cryptocurrencies, Explained. Cointelegraph, on December 13, 2017.

[20] **The DAO** was a digital decentralized autonomous organization, and a form of investor-directed venture capital fund. The DAO had an objective to provide a new decentralized business model for organizing both commercial and non-profit enterprises. It was instantiated on the Ethereum blockchain, and had no conventional management structure or board of directors. The code of the DAO is open-source. The DAO was stateless and not tied to any particular nation state. As a result, many questions of how government regulators would deal with a stateless fund were yet to be dealt with. The DAO was crowdfunded via a token sale in May 2016. It set the record for the largest crowdfunding campaign in history.

In June 2016, users exploited a vulnerability in the DAO code to enable them to siphon off one third of The DAO's funds to a subsidiary account. On 20 July 2016 01:20:40 PM +UTC at Block 1920000, the Ethereum community decided to hard-fork the Ethereum blockchain to restore virtually all funds to the original contract. This was controversial, and led to a fork in Ethereum, where the original unforked blockchain was maintained as Ethereum Classic, thus breaking Ethereum into two separate active blockchains, each with its own cryptocurrency. Wikipedia, In: *The DAO (organization)*.

What are cryptocurrencies?

Hence, from what has been said above, it is possible to conclude that:

They are not issue by any government. The fluctuation of its price is only linked to demand and supply.

Cryptocurrencies, which has a **private nature**, are issued and guaranteed by **cryptographics algorithms** (by mathematics and encryption). Cryptocurrencies are **decentralized** and they are executed via **Blockchain**[21] (Revoredo, 2018).

Thus, cryptocurrencies are a new asset (digital and with global range) that has enabled the development of a new Economy: The Crypto Economy.[22]

---

[21] To learn more about what Blockchain is, it is advisable to read: 1) "Blockchain and its potential to impact society and create unimaginable business models", 2) "DLT vs. Blockchain: brief comparative analysis of its underlying resources", both articles published on Global Blockchain Strategy.

[22] Idem Reference 11

What is Crypto Economy?

The crypto economy is a new way of doing business that uses crypto assets and decentralized protocols as facilitators of production, distribution, and consumption of goods and services in a digital and decentralized world (Revoredo, 2018).

"Possible" classifications of cryptocurrencies and their impact

There is a multiplicity of legal classifications attributed to Bitcoin and Cryptocurrencies, and, just mentioning some of them: commodities, financial assets, services, goods, financial instruments, means of payment, currency, e-money, private property, payment system, monetary substitute and unit of account (Fobe, 2016, pp. 70-74).

This diversity in cryptocurrencies classification is also reflected in its regulation, which has fluctuated substantially.

The legality of cryptocurrencies varies substantially from one country to another and is still undefined or changing in many others. While some countries explicitly authorized their use and exchange, others restricted or even banned them. Similarly, various government agencies, departments, and courts classify Bitcoin in different ways.

Some States **already accept and recognize cryptocurrencies with security**, while others **only express themselves positively** on the subject. There are those that **do not wish to interfere**, and those that **only expressed their fears**.

There are also skeptics about the quality of cryptocurrencies as enduring, and those that categorically **do not recognize their existence**.

Finally, some governments **want, or are about to, ban them** in their territory, and others that **have already banned them** (Revoredo, 2017).

On the other hand, in addition to numerous possible classifications, it can be seen that cryptocurrencies have been classified in more than one category within the same country: financial assets in Australia, Brazil and Bulgaria); immaterial asset in Australia, Singapore, the Netherlands and Norway; money in Australia, e-money in Lebanon; financial instrument in Germany and Norway; means of payment in Germany, the United Kingdom and Switzerland; Germany, Canada, the United States, Finland, Hong Kong, Ireland and Sweden; currency in the United States and Ireland; virtual currency in Croatia;

private property in France; service in Singapore, Finland, France and Poland; payment system in Spain; monetary substitute in Russia and unit of account in Austria (Fobe, 2016, pp. 70-74).

Hence, the conclusion that the current lack of regulation of cryptocurrencies derives from the difficulty of legislators to qualify the essence of cryptocurrencies and understand the extent of their impact on society.

Let us see, then, how governments, authorities and countries have positioned themselves.

CHAPTER 2 |
CRYPTOCURRENCIES
ECOSYSTEM AND ITS
CHALLENGES

Introduction

Despite the evolution of international scenario over the years, with growing interest of people [23] and the more attentive and serious look of governments [24] on

---

[23] As detailed in the "Search Year 2017" by research giant Google (GOOGLE, 2017), which gives an overview of what happened in 2017, bitcoin ranked second in the "Global News" category. Likewise, *How to Buy Bitcoin* also took third place in the "How ..." search category. With this, it is anticipated how strong was the attention and interest about bitcoin and cryptocurrencies, in 2017.

[24] Faced with the historic race in crypto-market prices in 2017, when the price of bitcoin grew 20x throughout the year, rising from about US$ 900 in January 2017 to a peak of US$ 19,783 in December of the same year. Crypto-currency market capitalization also surpassed US$ 650 billion, up from $ 17 billion since early January, according to CoinMarketCap (CoinMarketCap, 2018).

the subject, there is still a long way to go until some cryptocurrencies become global.

Therefore, in order to facilitate the understanding of cryptocurrencies ecosystem in the worldwide scenario, we will see in this topic: obstacles to the adoption of cryptocurrencies by people [25] and the biggest challenges found by legislators.

Obstacles to *mainstream* [26]

Nowadays, the biggest obstacle to the adoption of cryptocurrencies is undoubtedly the embryonic stage in which they are.

And like everything new, the difficulties range from cultural barriers, aspects of tax policy, concern with combating money laundering and protecting consumers.

---

[25] What is known in popular jargon as mainstream (mass adoption, ultimate goal of crypto-coins)

[26] Mainstream is the dominant trend or the most common or generalized current of thought in the context of a given culture. Dominant current includes all popular culture and mass culture, which are spread by mass media (WIKIPEDIA - The free encyclopedia, 2018).

So, let's look at these challenges to the adoption of cryptocurrencies one by one.

Cultural barriers

Cultural barriers are among the greatest challenges to the widespread adoption of cryptocurrencies, due to lack of understanding of general public about new technologies.

The fact is, not everyone is *"early adopter"* and is willing to entrust their money to a *"faceless"* computer system, especially if they cannot easily deal with technology.

In addition, in their current stage of development, cryptocurrencies still require some knowledge and study by those who wish to acquire them, for example, it is necessary to learn about how public and private keys work. Well, for mass adoption, cryptocurrencies have to reach sufficient technological maturity for their "easy use".

Moreover, the reputation of bitcoin acquired in the days of *"Silk Road"*[27], coupled with media not

---

[27] Silk Road was a market that operated through Darknet and used Tor network to thereby ensure anonymity of buyers and sellers in illicit trade, particularly narcotics. The site was

specialized in the subject, contributed to increase confusion of those who have difficulty in understanding, or are not open to new technologies.

Tax policy

Security of personal privacy provided by cryptocurrencies encryption, which makes difficult to trace their use by authorities, could eliminate or require a change in current tax policy. And a significant part of this realignment of currency and underlying tax system would impact governments and current private sector entities that provide currency storage and transaction services (central or private banks), credit card payment systems, etc.) (Walton, 2014).

---

launched in February 2011 (Norrie & Moses, 2011). As of 2012, annual sales were estimated at 22 million US dollars (Christin, 2012). In October 2013, FBI closed the site [6] and arrested Ross William Ulbricht, accusing him of being "Dread Pirate Roberts" or DPR, the site owner (Anderson & Farivar, 2013). On November 6, 2013, Silk Road 2.0 was launched by former Silk Road managers (Greenberg, 2013). This was also closed, and his alleged operator was arrested on November 6, 2014, in the so-called "Operation Onymous", international police operation against Darknet markets and other obscure services in Tor network. Ulbricht was sentenced to life imprisonment (Weiser, 2015).

Thus, it is reasonable to expect resistance and recognition of cryptocurrency value and feasibility by those who hold the power.

Anti-Money Laundry (AML)

The second obstacle to adoption lies in the association, by authorities and legislators, of using cryptocurrencies for practice of fraud and money laundering.

In this field, one can see a global and continuous narrative of international governments that money laundering is fundamental battleground for harder regulation of cryptocurrencies.

In face of this, many governments have closely watched their sphere of cryptocurrencies brokers, subjecting them to periodic inspections and KYC procedures, "Know Your Client"[28].

At this year's World Economic Forum, for example, the US Treasury Secretary said his focus is on ensuring that cryptocurrencies are not used for illicit

---

[28] That translated literally would be "Know your client": one of the standard rules of any compliance program in a large financial institution

activities, while Theresa May expressed concern that criminals may use cryptocurrencies to anonymous transferring of resources[29].

In Japan, on the other hand, reports informing suspicious situations began to be required in April 2017, after new legislation required Cryptocurrencies brokerage firms to be more transparent and compliant with anti-money laundering regulations. Despite the continuing narrative by international governments that money laundering is the central reason for cryptocurrencies to be subject to tougher regulations, figures are promising. Only 0.16% of the transactions reported in money-laundering reports in 2017 came from cryptocurrency operations (Suberg, 2018).

Other countries, on the other hand, are considering to base cryptocurrency regulations on existing trading rules for gold and derivatives, in order to prevent cryptocurrencies from being used for money laundering (Groendahl, 2018).

There is also a movement by some authorities, such as the Austrian Finance Minister, to form a working group, together with the European Union Commission in Brussels, to accept proposals from

---

[29] Event that I attended, held in Davos within January 23 and 26 2018

member countries on how to deal with cryptocurrency fraud (Vietnna.AT, 2018).

Here, it is important to remember there are companies, like Chainalysis[30] and Elliptic[31], that perform cryptocurrency tracking, and help prevent, detect and investigate cryptocurrencies money laundering, fraud and compliance violations.

Securities regulators

When it comes to cryptocurrencies, securities and capital market authorities are having serious

---

[30] Chainalysis is a compliance and research software for the world's top institutions. Its Blockchain Intelligence Platform is able to cryptocurrency transaction monitoring in real-time with raises real-time alerts on incoming and outgoing transactions for links to potentially suspicious activity. Its compliance analysts get dynamically updated customer risk profiles with the most up to date information from the blockchain for periodic reviews. Also, Chainalysis uses pattern recognition, machine learning and millions of open source references to identify and categorize 1,000's of cryptocurrency services.

[31] Elliptic identify illicit activity in cryptocurrencies, providing actionable intelligence to cryptocurrency companies, financial institutions and government agencies.

difficulties in understanding and interpreting their reflexes in capital markets structure.

While some jurisdictions have acted with caution, due to innovation inherent in this new model of instrument, still in constant evolution as regards its economic and legal nature, other jurisdictions have acted with excessive rigor, as is the case, for example, in the State of Israel, whose chairman of Securities and Exchange Commission[32] has expressed his wish to ban Tel Aviv Stock Exchange listed companies, which want to have their businesses based on Bitcoin or other cryptocurrencies (Scheer, 2017).

Concerns range from the best practices in cryptocurrencies derivative market (which can be considered in some cases as securities, depending therefore on regulator's authorization to be offered to the public) to the lack of regulation for ICOs[33] public

---

[32] ISA, in the English acronym

[33] Public offer of Cryptocurrencies, public funding of resources, having in contrast issuance of virtual assets (also known as tokens or coins), with investing public. Here, it is important to note, however, that there are ICO transactions that are not under the jurisdiction of securities authorities, since they do not constitute public offerings of securities.

33

offers of cryptocurrencies and trading exchanges (brokerage firms), among others

For this reason, cryptocurrencies have presented a huge challenge to securities regulators, which, therefore, hampers their global adoption.

CHAPTER 3 | CENTRAL BANKS REACTION TO THE CRYPTOCURRENCIES

Introduction

In a country, Central Bank controls the supplying of money through a set of tools (the so-called monetary policy) that directly and indirectly influences the supply or demand of money.

Nearly ten years since Bitcoin's birth, Central Banks around the world have sought to understand the advantages and disadvantages of cryptocurrencies. Recently, BIS, considered the Central Bank of Central Banks, said lawmakers cannot ignore the growth of cryptocurrencies.

Faced with this, here is an outline of how the world's largest central banks have positioned themselves in relation to cryptocurrencies.

Central Banks now face a new challenge

The sudden rise of cryptocurrencies may pose challenges to central banks and financial intermediaries alike. At least these are their fans' hopes and targets: to create private currencies that compete successfully with the official fiat currencies and disrupt business models of banks (Fatás & Di Mauro, 2018).

The introduction of parallel currencies (cryptocurrencies) can have an effect on the operations of central banks at many levels (Fernández-Villaverde and Sanches 2016). There is an analogy between this situation and the case of central banks dealing with partial dollarization of their economies (Baliño et al. 1999).

First, if transactions in the new currency are widespread, it might make it impossible for the central bank to find appropriate intermediate targets for its monetary policy. Second, as individuals, corporations, and possible financial institutions increase their holdings of the new currency, it can potential make the financial system less stable unless the central bank can find ways to stabilise liquidity in those currencies. Finally, it can induce additional uncertainty and volatility in the exchange rate (Calvo and Vegh 1992).

This is why many authorities have seen crypto-coins as a threat to the monopoly of monetary policy.

As Central Banks are positioning themselves on cryptocurrencies

Reserve Bank of Australia (RBA)

In a speech in Sydney, shortly after the launch of CME Group's[34] first bitcoin futures market, Philip Lowe, Reserve Bank of Australia (RBA) chief, said it was difficult to see bitcoins being used for daily transactions.

Lowe noted that "(...) *as a payment instrument, it seems more attractive to those who want to do black market or illegal transactions, rather than everyday transactions."* The value of bitcoin is very volatile, the number of payments that can be currently managed is very low, there are governance issues, the transaction cost involved to make a payment with bitcoin is very high and the estimates of electricity*

---

[34] To take advantage of growing investor interest, Chicago-based derivatives brokerage, CBOE Global Markets began trading futures on bitcoins on Sunday while CME Group began its contracts on December 17, 2017.

used in mining process are surprising"(Pandey & Cole, 2017).

He added that the Australian central bank is open to the idea of issuing a new form of digital money, perhaps using distributed accounting technology in which bitcoins work, but stressed that there are no immediate plans to issue an Australian dollar electronic currency, since the history of private issuance is of periodic panic and instability.

Despite Philip Lowe's speech in 2017, Tony Richards, head of the RBA's payment policy department, dismissed the idea of issuing a "central bank digital currency - CBDCs" due to low demand (Zhao, 2018).

Central Bank of Brazil (BACEN)

When defining what "virtual coins" are, the Central Bank of Brazil (BACEN in a Portuguese acronym) does so in a similar way to the one adopted by the New York State Regulatory Framework, drawn up in the same period.

The Central Bank of Brazil names cryptocurrencies as "virtual coins" or "encrypted coins" and differentiates it from electronic currencies.

Electronic Coins are resources stored in an electronic device or system that allows the end user to carry out a payment transaction in national currency.

Regulated by Law 12,865/2013, electronic coins comprise, for instance, the digital units of pre-paid credit cards and the coins used in gaming platforms.

Cryptocurrencies, called by BACEN as "virtual currencies," have their own form, that is, they are distinct units of account of currencies issued by sovereign governments.

The Central Bank of Brazil is accurate in the diagnosis when it shows itself conscious and attentive to the private nature of cryptocurrencies (Revoredo, 2017).

In relation to the banking regulation of cryptocurrencies, BACEN issued Communiqué No. 25,306, dated 2/19/2014, whose simple and succinct content tells us that the number of transactions of "virtual currencies" in Brazil is still very low. Therefore, its use still does not pose risks to the National Financial System, especially considering the volume purchases in the retail.

Regarding the guarantee of conversion of the cryptocurrencies to "Real", BACEN pointed out that there is no guarantee of conversion to the official currency, nor they are guaranteed by real assets of any kind.

Also, The Central Bank of Brazil clarified that the value of converting an cryptocurrency to currencies issued by monetary authorities depends on the credibility and confidence that market agents have in accepting the so-called virtual currency as a medium of exchange and expectations of its appreciation. There is, therefore, no governmental mechanism that guarantees the official value of the cryptocurrencies. That's why all risk of their acceptance is in the hands of users.

Central Bank of Canada

Carolyn Wilkins, Senior Vice Governor of Bank of Canada, is leading research on cryptography and said in November that cryptocurrencies are not real forms of money. *"This is really an asset, or a security, and so it should be treated that way"*, Wilkins said. Like others, she considered the technology of distributed books as promising to make the financial system more efficient. BOC team is also exploring the circumstances in which it may be appropriate for the bank to issue its own digital currency.

China Monetary Authority

China made clear: the central bank has full control over cryptocurrencies. With a research team set up in 2014 to develop digital fiat money, People's Bank of China believes that *"conditions are ripe"* for it to embrace the technology. But at the same time, authorities are attacking mining operations and Cryptocurrencies like Bitcoin. China says that becoming digital could help improving the efficiency of means of payment and enable more accurate control of currencies.

Denmarks National Bank

Denmarks National Bank, in a study published late last year, concluded that the introduction of digital currency issued by the country's monetary authority would not result in better payment solutions and could also pose risks of financial instability.

> "In the Danish context, it is not clear what the central bank's digital currency could contribute that is not yet covered by current payment solutions, "noting that Denmark has a secure and effective payment infrastructure which, among other things, provides for immediate settlement of payments and includes guarantees for bank deposits up to about kr. 750,000"[35] (News - Danmarks National Bank, 2017)

---

[35] Free Translation of: "In a Danish context, it is unclear what central bank digital currency would be able to contribute that is not

41

Well, that is why the head of Denmarks Nationalbank told investors to "stay away" from bitcoin. In a statement at the end of last year, Lars Rohde (director of Denmarks Nationalbank) pointed out that it is not a regulated market, so it is not responsibility of authorities and, therefore, users are fully responsible for their actions, as well as they cannot complain if something goes wrong (DR, 2017).

Bank of England – BOE

UK Central Bank - BOE Bank of England - is aware that the world is in a potential "revolution" in financial market and sees Blockchain technology - accounting distributed database - as a great promise to allow central banks strengthen their defenses against cyber-attacks, and review how payments are made between institutions and consumers. However, it is far from creating a digital version of UK pound.

---

already covered by the current payment solutions," the analysis states, pointing out that Denmark has a secure and effective payments infrastructure which, among other things, provides for immediate settlement of payments and includes guarantees for bank deposits up to approximately kr. 750,000.

As for cryptocurrencies, Mark Carney - chairman of Bank of England - said that bitcoin faces regulatory repression and that cryptocurrencies are failing to fulfill their basic function as currency.

Still, on the current situation of cryptocurrency negotiations, with market growing rapidly in unregulated exchanges, Carney said in a speech in early March that although bitcoin and other cryptocurrencies do not seem to pose material risks to financial stability, this may change in future as more people begin to use them, so it is time to "regulate the elements of cryptocurrencies ecosystem to combat illicit activities." (The Guardian - International Edition, 2018).

European Central Bank and Euro Zone

European Central Bank has repeatedly warned about the dangers of investing in digital currencies.

Vice-President Vitor Constancio said in September 2017 that Bitcoin is not a currency, but a "tulip" - alluding to the seventeenth-century bubble in the Netherlands.

ECB President Mario Draghi said in November that the impact of digital currencies on economy of Euro area was limited.

At the World Economic Forum in Davos in January this year, Benoît Couré - a member of the Executive

Board and responsible for policies of the European Central Bank – warned[36] that the leaders of the world's largest economies planned to discuss a global regulatory framework for cryptocurrencies at the meeting of G20 Summit in March, in the city of Buenos Aires, as happened later. And, in a surprising moment of his speech, Benoît Couré questioned "How do you understand and how do you control these gateways between the obscure monetary universe and the regular financial system?" [37]and then stated, "This is being discussed and there will be answers."[38]

Still, in a speech directed at policymakers, Benoîte Couré said that opportunities presented by cryptocurrencies[22] (...), should not be lost sight of, and added [39], "... *what Bitcoin tells us as central bankers is that our payment systems are very*

---

[36] In a speech to which I was present, held in Davos (on 26/1/2018)

[37] Literal translation of his original speech: "How do you understand and how do you control these gateways between the shadow currency universe and the regular financial system?"

[38] Literal translation of his original speech: "That's being discussed and there will be answers"

[39] Literal translation of his original speech: "But don't lose sight of the opportunities"

expensive and very slow, and we have to act on it, and we need better cross-border payments because it is good for development and that is good for financial inclusion"[40]

Central Bank of Finland

A document released on Sept. 5 by the Bank of Finland's Research Department - Central Bank of Finland[41] - recognized Bitcoin's economic system as a "revolutionary system."

Developed by three researchers at Columbia Business School (Huberman, Leshno, & Moallemi, 2017), after research on the pros and cons of bitcoin infrastructure, research points to bitcoin technology as a "monopoly run by a protocol whose dynamics offers a degree of protection against eventual manipulation of the market.

---

[40] Literal translation of his original speech: "(...) what Bitcoin tells us as central bankers is that our payments systems are too expensive and too slow, and we have got to act on that and we need better cross-border payments because it is good for development and it is good for financial inclusion".

[41] It is the fourth oldest central bank in the world

And among other notable statements presented throughout the paper, authors note that there is no need to regulate bitcoin because, as a system, it commits itself to the protocol, and transaction fees it charges are determined by users, regardless of miners efforts.

Although the document itself indicates that the points of view presented do not represent Bank of Finland official position, the publication is undoubtedly remarkable because of central bank's involvement with the technology to date

Central Bank of France

In the statement made in Beijing (Galhau, 2017), François Villeroy from Galhau, president of Central Bank of France, stood as follows:

> "I would like to say a few words about bitcoin, which is a subject of great attention, especially here in China. It is associated with a useful technology, that of blockchain and distributed records (or Distributed Ledger Technology). Banque de France, like other players, is experimenting this innovative technology.
>
> But in addition, there should be no ambiguity: bitcoin is not a currency,

not even a cryptocurrency. It is a speculative asset. Its value and high volatility do not correspond to any economic underpinnings and is not responsibility of anyone. Banque de France would like to point out that those who invest in bitcoins do so entirely at their own risk.

We also noted with interest the measures taken by Chinese authorities regarding ICOs."[42]

---

[42] Literal translation of: "Je voudrais d'abord dire quelques mots sur le bitcoin, sujet de grande attention particulièrement ici en Chine. Il est associé à une technologie utile, celle de la blockchain et des registres distribués (ou Distributed Ledger Technology). La Banque de France, comme d'autres acteurs, expérimente cette technologie innovante. Mais au-delà, il ne doit pas y avoir d'ambiguïté : le bitcoin n'est en rien une monnaie, ou même une crypto monnaie. C'est un actif spéculatif. Sa valeur et sa forte volatilité ne correspondent à aucun sous-jacent économique et ne sont la responsabilité de personne. La Banque de France tient à rappeler que ceux qui investissent en bitcoin le font totalement à leurs risques et périls. Nous avons noté par ailleurs avec intérêt les mesures prises par les autorités chinoises concernant les ICO."

Reserve Bank of India – RBI

India's monetary authority has been opposing cryptocurrencies on the grounds that they violate foreign exchange rules and are a channel for money laundering and terrorist financing. Taking a firm stand on the subject, Reserve Bank of India (RBI) has issued notices in 2013 (RBI - Reserve Bank of India, 2013) and 2017 (RBI - Reserve Bank of India, 2017), in which it warns "users, owners and merchants "that it had not authorized any company in India to provide services related to cryptocurrencies.

Bank of Japan (BOJ)

Although investment in Bitcoin is popular in Japan, Bank of Japan adopts cautious stance on cryptocurrencies

In its official website, the Japanese monetary authority has published a page called "*Let's Think About Cryptocurrencies!*" Aimed at general public, the website includes questions such as: Can cryptocurrencies be considered as money? Is it possible to profit from them? and Are they likely to be stolen? (Sheridan, 2018).

Haruhiko Kuroda, chairman of Bank of Japan (BOJ), had already expressed concern about cryptocurrencies, and Finance Ministers and leaders of the G20 central banks (Group of 20) at the summit held in March this year, were concerned about whether cryptocurrencies could destabilize financial markets (Takeo, 2018).

BOJ Questions and Answers, published earlier this year on a financial education website, provide a basic overview of cryptocurrencies, explaining how they are different from traditional currencies, noting that there is no central bank to back them up, and details on how you do not necessarily profit by investing in them. On the website, there are answers to various questions, such as how useful and profitable virtual currencies are, how their value is determined, what points to consider when investing in virtual currencies, among others (The Central Council For Financial Services Information, 2018).

Central Bank of Mexico

Mexico's central bank governor, Agustin Carstens, rejects the legal classification of "virtual currency" for Bitcoin and, in a local report, said that bitcoin should be considered a commodity. And arguing that bitcoin is not supported by a government or central bank, Carstens asserted that cryptocurrency does not meet the existing definitions of currency (Morales, 2017).

During a lecture at Technical University of Mexico, ITAM, governor emphasized the role of authorities, saying that "*technological development in the financial system cannot be the result of innovation alone*", but should occur in conjunction with regulation of financial authorities.

Central Bank of Nigeria – CBN

Central Bank of Nigeria, maintaining its stance since 2015 (Perez, 2015), issued a new statement in early 2018 (CBN, 2018) to alert its residents and Nigerian financial institutions about the lack of security of cryptocurrencies, as well as about possible risks. The alert also says that cryptocurrency trading platforms, such as NairaEx - Nigeria-based bitcoin brokerage - "*are not licensed or regulated by CBN.*"

The statement follows previous messages [43] [44] [45] sent to Nigerian financial institutions in early 2017, in which Nigerian monetary authority advised domestic

---

[43]

https://www.cbn.gov.ng/Out/2017/FPRD/AML%20January%202017%20Circular%20to%20FIs%20on%20Virtual%20Currency.pdf

[44]   https://www.coindesk.com/nigerias-central-bank-calls-for-bitcoin-regulation/

[45] Nigerian Securities and Exchange Commission (SEC): http://sec.gov.ng/public-notice-on-investments-in-cryptocurrencies-and-other-virtual-or-digital-currencies/

banks to distance themselves from cryptocurrencies, warning them to "*not use, maintain or otherwise transact with said technology.*"

It is important to note, however, that such alerts occur at a time when Nigeria is experiencing growing interest in cryptocurrency market, with weekly trading volume in Localbitcoins exchange increasing by 500% in 2017 (Zhao, 2018).

Central Bank of the Philippines

The Central Bank of the Philippines (BSP) introduced legislation to recognize and regulate crypto-currency trading exchanges in early 2017, seeking to create a regulatory apparatus that promotes innovation, while managing risks related to money laundering and financing of terrorism.

Espenilla described bitcoin as enjoying significant recent growth in the Philippines, claiming that trading volume almost tripled in 12 months[46]. BSP governor further emphasized "the importance" of bitcoin negotiations "under the state's regulatory framework", and expressed his belief that virtual currencies have potential to revolutionize payments

---

[46] average monthly trading volume of US$ 6 million in 2017, compared to only US$ 2 million in 2016.

51

and financial services industries, suggesting that it can promote greater financial inclusion regarding virtual monetary industries in the future (Agcaoili, 2017)

Central Bank of Russia

Central Bank of Russia expressed concern about potential risks of cryptocurrencies; President Elvira Nabiullina said that "we do not legalize pyramid schemes" and "we are totally opposed to private money, whether in physical or virtual form." For now, Bank of Russia prefers to postpone a decision on regulation of cryptocurrencies, unless President Vladimir Putin acts earlier.

Here, it should be noted that the President of Russian Federation Central Bank has a position opposed to the Russian Minister of Finance, who has already presented a Law for Regulation of Digital Assets, which defines and establishes a regulatory system for cryptocurrencies, ICOs, mining and trade.

Monetary Authority of Singapore (MAS)

Head of central bank of Singapore (known as MAS, Monetary Authority of Singapore), Ravi Menon, is not convinced that central banks should create their own cryptocurrencies, and recently said that the ambition of Singapore to become a global technology center has its limits, because financial stability is above economic development. In an interview with the Financial Times, in his office, in Singapore, Mr. Menon said:

> "What does [central banks issuing digital currency to nonbanking public] mean? It means that you and I will have cryptocurrencies deposits in the cloud, with a private key issued by central bank. Whose responsibility is it? It is central bank's responsibility directly to the individual. Why does central bank want to do this? If there is any nervousness in the banks, you will have a run on the bank; everyone will go to central bank [with their deposits]... And if people deposited their money in central banks, who would provide credit? " (Menon, 2018).

That is why MAS is assessing if additional regulations are needed to protect investors in cryptocurrencies (Reuters, 2018).

Central Bank of South Korea

South Korean officials focused on protecting consumers and preventing cryptography from being used as a crime tool. While government continues to weigh legislation to terminate encryption exchanges, the country's Financial Services Commission is creating a special team to investigate cryptography trade. South Korea is set up to start a real-name account system for this negotiation. Deputy Governor of Bank of Korea, Shin Hosoon, said in November 2017 that more research and monitoring was needed. Many Koreans embraced Bitcoin. Korean Prime Minister warned that cryptography could corrupt the nation's youth.

Central Bank of Turkey

Digital currencies may contribute to financial stability if well designed, said the head of Central Bank of Turkey, Murat Cetinkaya, in Istanbul in November. But they pose new risks to central banks, including controlling money supply, price stability, and transmission of monetary policy, Cetinkaya said. Even so, Turkish central banker said that crypto-coins can be an important element for a cashless economy, and technologies can help accelerate and make payment systems more efficient (Lam, 2017).

U.S. Central Bank (Federal Reserve)

The posture of The Federal Reserve on cryptocurrencies is in its infancy and shows a concern for privacy. Jerome Powell, current president of *The Federal Reserve*, addressed at the beginning of last year some technical issues that permeate blockchain technology and even said that "risk management and governance will be critical" (Powell, 2017).

See below the main passages of his speech in *The Yale Law School Center for the Study of Corporate Law*, in New Haven, Connecticut.

In addressing the new DLT (Decentralized Ledger Technology) technology, Powell stated that:

> "And as with any new technology, things can go wrong. We will need a thorough review of how DLT fits into current legal milestones and which gaps need to be met by contractual agreements or new laws and regulations. A robust legal basis that provides certainty in relevant jurisdictions is essential for building strong governance, risk management and operations" (Powell, 2017).

Then, regarding central bank issuance of digital coins, after highlighting "significant" technical challenges, and the privacy issue as a problem, Powell noted that while this is a fascinating notion, there are important policy issues that need to be analyzed, such as:

> A digital currency would also be a major target as a potential vehicle for

global criminal activity, including money laundering.

Advanced encryption could reduce vulnerability to cyber-attacks but facilitate concealment of illegal activities.

Increasing computing power over time can be used to increase security but can also increase threats.

Privacy issues should be seriously considered. Central banks would have to maintain digital currency issuance records and may need to keep individual transaction records to authenticate these transactions and combat cyber risks and illegal activities. In today's environment, commercial banks maintain extensive records for individual transactions with debit and credit cards and are increasingly monitoring fraud behavior patterns. However, such records in the hands of a central bank or a government entity may raise serious privacy concerns on the part of users and may limit public appeal.

Any central bank that is actively thinking of issuing its own digital currency would need to carefully consider the full range of payment system and other political issues that appear to be substantial, as well as potential social benefits. In my opinion, they should also consider whether the private sector can substantially meet the same needs.

Finally, Powell concluded:

"We live in a time of extraordinary technological change. We must be open to new ideas and innovations that will drive economic growth and improvements in our financial system. At the same time, public is rightly waiting for authorities to do whatever it takes to keep their money safe. We, the public sector, shall insist on security and protection, while working to ensure that our citizens benefit from payment system innovation." (Powell, 2017)

BIS

BIS - known as the Central Bank of Central Banks - used its quarterly report to discuss cryptocurrencies, such as Bitcoin and Ethereum. It warned that the monetary authorities of the countries can no longer ignore the growth of cryptocurrencies and will probably have to consider issuing their own digital currencies in the near future, suggesting that one option would be making a currency available to the public with exclusive issuance of said units by the central bank, directly convertible into cash and reserves (Bech & Garratt, 2017).

And, at the end of the report, it concludes that **central banks will have to consider not only consumer preferences as to privacy and possible efficiency gains** - in terms of payments, clearing and settlement - **but also the risks** that this may entail for the financial system and economy in general, as well as any implications for monetary policy (Bordo & Levin, 2017).

CHAPTER 4 |
GOVERNMENTS AND
CRYPTOCURRENCIES

Introduction

Cryptocurrencies legislation has widely varied from country to country, although this may change with recent global coordination among G20 members, as we will see at the end of this topic. In this topic, you will be shown an overview on how key governments and authorities have dealt with cryptocurrencies.

Australia

On July 1, 2017, Australia officially recognized Bitcoin and other cryptocurrencies "as money" and would no longer be subject to double taxation thereafter. Also, in its budget summary for 2017-18, the Australian government states that:

"Government will make it easier for new digital currency companies to operate in Australia." (...) "As of July 1, 2017, digital currency purchases will no longer be subject to GST, allowing digital currencies to be treated as money for tax purposes. Currently, consumers who use digital currencies are subject to double taxation: once in the purchase of digital currency and once again in its use in the exchange for other goods and services subject to GST." (Government of Australia, 2017).

Aiming at strengthening cryptocurrencies industry and extinguish criminal activity, Australia has just passed a law that has introduced additional regulation of cryptocurrencies ecosystem, requiring service providers to adopt the new guidelines introduced by AUSTRAC, Australian Center for Transaction Analysis (Australian Government - AUSTRAC, 2018).

The new regulation is very similar to the way FSA (Financial Services Agency) of Japan approaches the cryptocurrencies sector (The Straits Times, 2018). Anyone who does not register with AUSTRAC will be violating the new regulation, and companies must comply with governmental requirements of AML and CTF (Anti-Money Laundering and Terrorist

Financing), which also includes reporting strange activities occurring on their respective platforms.

The Australian regulatory agency seeks to better understand how cryptocurrencies have been used in Australia by adopting an open positioning with appropriate taxation guidelines for digital assets (Buntinx, 2018).

Brazil[47]

Brazil has excellent well-structured institutions, like the Federal Revenue, **Financial Activities Control Council ("COAF")** and the Central Bank. These agencies regulate and audit assets and similar services, such as national currency, its custody, and transactions. However, they supervise currencies issued by states, and not assets of private hybrid nature and already inspected by the users of the system themselves.

---

[47] Revoredo, T. In: Legal Status of Cryptocurrencies in Brazil, Medium, Submitted on Nov 6, 2017 (v1), last revised Apr 12, 2018 (this version, v2)

Federal Revenue of Brazil

Federal Revenue (RFB in a Portuguese acronym), in the questions and answers manual regarding the Tax Declaration 2017 (IRPF 2017), released every year, has directly treated the theme in its topic "447— Should virtual currency be declared?" The answer is "Yes. Virtual currencies (like Bitcoins, for instance), although not considered as money, as per the terms on the current regulatory mark, they must be declared on the form "Assets and Royalties" as 'other assets,' once they can be comparable to a financial asset."

Financial Activities Control Council ("COAF")

The Financial Activities Control Council ("COAF") (the leading governmental agency for the combat against money laundering in Brazil) positioned itself in favor of the regulation of digital money, like Bitcoin. That was at the third public hearing regarding the draft bill № 2303/2015, which took place in the Chamber of Deputies on September 17, 2017.

According to the initial proposal of Draft Law № 2303/2015, digital money would be included in the definition of payment arrangements under the regulatory responsibility of Central Bank, and inspection by COAF.

Cryptocurrencies and the legal treatment intended by the Brazilian Congress — The Draft Bill № 2.303/2015

An Special Committee at Brazil's Chamber of Deputies is currently discussing regulation about cryptocurrencies.

The Draft Bill № 2.303/2015, whose author is the Federal Deputy Mr. Aureo Ribeiro, intends to include virtual coins as well as frequent flyer programs in the definition of arrangements of payments, under the supervision of BACEN, with the explanation that a "prudential regulation" is necessary due to the risks of "monetary alternative to the drug dealing and money laundering."

The Congressman Mr. Expedito Neto has presented a substitute report to the rapporteur's report that intends to criminalize cryptocurrencies.

As another Congressman, Mr. Thiago Peixoto, understands that cryptocurrencies should be regulated considering also the possible benefits of these technologies to Brazil, he presented a third report's proposal about the subject.

Since 2015, public hearings have already taken place to debate such Draft Bill.

In 2017, there were important public hearings such as that happened on July 5, 2017 [1], with the presence of Fernando Ulrich, an economist specialized in Bitcoin, Marcelo Miranda, Executive Director of the Brazilian brokerage company FlowBTC, and Lázaro Jung Martins, undersecretary of Inspection of the Federal Revenue.

It is also important to mention the hearing held on August 30, 2017 [2], counted with the presence of the Counselor of the Department of Regulations of the Financial System of Central Bank of Brazil, Mr. Madilson Fernandes Queiroz. The attorney Ms. Helena Margarido, an expert in cryptocurrencies and blockchain; the Professor of Computer Science, Mr. João Gondim, from Universidade de Brasília; the Brazilian broker Mr., Bernardo Faria, partner-owner at Foxbit, and Ms. Taynaah Reis, co-founder of the Coin Project were also present.

On September 13, 2017, there was another important public hearing [3] happened with the presence of the Director of Financial Intelligence of the Financial Activities Control Council ("COAF"), of the representative of the Securities and Exchange Commission ("CVM"), and of the representative of the cryptocurrencies brokerage CoinBr.

Throughout the debates, the Brazilian public authorities referred mostly to the use of the protocol of crypto coins—in particular, of Bitcoin—as a payment system, for transferring of values, or for real investment. They focused on three points of attention arising from this technology:

> a) The systemic risk—an eventual failure of the software, which may negatively affect the confidence, what is mitigated for being a free open software, which is continuously being audited and improved;
>
> b) Market risk—for those who use bitcoin, as means of value transfer or investment, there is no guarantee over a bitcoin value once it is freely defined in the market
>
> c) Risk of usability—there is plenty hearsay regarding users who have lost their bitcoins for not performing a backup of the passwords or for merely forgetting them. [48]

When discussing the Draft Law 2303/2015, thus, one must keep in mind the idea behind the first cryptocurrency, Bitcoin (or, "web currency," or "the Internet coin," as some prefer), and the Blockchain technology (its decentralized architecture in a peer-to-peer network.

---

[48] Ulrich, Fernando. In: "Discurso proferido em Brasília, na Audiência pública de 5/7/2017".

"The cryptocurrencies and blockchain structures as a system go way beyond a simple means of payment. That is because they came to solve something much more prominent, the problems about the current centralized method of transferring and the financial intermediation (intermediation costs, privacy, security, double spending, among others) and the obstacles related to every model based on reliance.

The dimension of the changes brought about by cryptocurrencies is still far from being wholly unveiled.

The array of possible uses increases every day. That is why it is reckless a legal proposal that intends to regulate the market of cryptocurrencies with the same measures (and weight) applied to the means of payment."[49]

Canada

Canada is preparing to regulate and become a global center for cryptocurrencies sector.

---

[49] Idem Reference 47

Amendments to Money Laundering and Terrorism Financing Act (PCMLTF), approved in 2014, but not yet in force, will require Cryptocurrency brokers to register with Federal Financial Intelligence Unit (FINTRAC), as well as implement an anti-money laundering compliance regime. Furthermore, banks will be prohibited from providing services to companies unregistered with FINTRAC as well (Faife, 2018).

China

China is poised to increase prohibitions on cryptocurrency brokers and initial currency offerings (ICOs) (Jia, 2018), by increasing monitoring of cryptocurrency accounts as well as supervision of foreign currency flows in ICOs abroad (Reuters, 2018). Such measures aim at ending the entire trade in cryptocurrencies.

While China's government intends with repression reduce Chinese participation in cryptocurrency markets, this intolerant stance has not gotten the effect expected by Chinese authorities.

Rather, in September 2017, Chinese government, the People's Bank of China (PBoC) and local financial regulators imposed a national ban on Cryptocurrencies and ICOs (Initial Coin Offering), something similar to the IPO on the stock exchanges (BBC, 2017).

The global cryptocurrency exchange market, however, has restructured while most volumes traded in China and new ICO proposals have shifted to neighboring markets (such as Japan, for example) with efficient and well-regulated ecosystems compared to China. Not to mention significant increase in trading volumes of Over-the-Counter (OTC) and *peer-to-peer* (P2P) trading platforms.

Now the Chinese are trading cryptocurrencies and exchanging Chinese yuan without control and supervision of local authorities. To understand the Chinese Cryptocurrencies Market, it is interesting to read the article published in the Markets section of Business Insider website, 9/16/2017, by Tama Churchouse, whose title translated would be *"China's repression will not kill Cryptocurrencies - but it will have an impact. "*

As we can draw from the Chinese case, elaboration of a new regulation of technologies still under construction, applying inadequate legal frameworks to them, is actually ineffective (Revoredo, 2018).

Denmark

In 2014, Danish government stated that bitcoin was not money in the true sense of the word, as it is not supported by an issuing institution (Hajdarbegovic, 2014).

The director of Denmark Financial Supervisory Authority (Finanstilsynets direktør), Jesper Berg, pointed out late last year that there may be a need to establish rules for bitcoins if their popularity increases in the country. He says that today there are practically no rules for the new phenomenon that otherwise happens in known financial markets, with stocks and bonds, and complements:

> "If all of a sudden people really start moving into this universe, then we should also start thinking about how we regulate them, so it's not going wrong for them"[50] (DR, 2017).

Estonia

Estonian Supreme Court ruled on April 4, 2016, that the trading of cryptocurrencies is a legitimate trading activity, governed by the Anti-Money Laundering Law and the Financing Terrorism Law. In the same process[51], it clarified that for a cryptocurrency broker

---

[50] Free translation of: "Hvis det pludselig er sådan at folk for alvor begynder at bevæge sig ud i det univers, så må vi også begynde at tænke på, hvordan regulerer vi det, sådan at det ikke går alt for galt for dem"

[51] Procedure n° 3-3-1-75-15

to operate, applicant must obtain an authorization (known as Alternative Payment Media Provider) of Financial Intelligence Unit (in Estonian: Rahapesu Andmebüroo) (Loban, 2018).

Almost a year and a half after this emblematic decision, the **Estonian Parliament** enacted a new version of Anti-Money Laundering and Terrorist Financing Law, aiming at addressing deficiencies in previous version, whose main highlights are:

1. A clear definition of cryptocurrencies ("virtual currencies")

2. Regulation of the Cryptocurrencies portfolios offer

3. Remote identification of customers for cryptocurrencies brokers and storage service providers

4. Possibility of delegating customer identification to a qualified third party

5. A new definition and significant expansion of duties of the person responsible for processing money laundering complaints

6. Obligation of regulated companies to develop sound risk management policies, considering their needs for risk, liquidity, capital and many other risk factors.

7. Heavy fines for non-compliance with standards

In the new law, more specifically in Section 3 (9), cryptocurrencies are called "virtual currencies" and are defined as follows:

> "Virtual currency" means a value represented in digital form, which is digitally transferable, preservable or negotiable and that natural or legal persons accept as instrument of payment, but which is not the legal currency of any country or funds for the purposes of Article 4, nº 25 of Directive (EU) 2015/2366 of the European Parliament and of Council on payment services in domestic market, amending Directives 2002/65 / EC, 2009/110 / EC and 2013/36 Regulation (EU) No 1093/2010 and repealing Directive 2007/64 / EC (OJ L 337, 23.12.2015, pp. 35-127) or a payment transaction for the purposes of points (k) e1) of Article 3 of that Directive."

The holder of a valid authorization to deal with virtual currency in Estonia, in turn, is known as *"provider of virtual currency exchange service for fiduciary currency"* (in Estonian: *Virtuaalvääringu raha vastu vahetamise teenuse pakkujad*), according to Section 2 (10) of the aforementioned law.

Digital assets are classified as property for tax purposes. Only cryptocurrency brokers are regulated.

In addition, Estonia's legal structure is built to attract investors from around the world, and the country is increasingly aware of cryptocurrency startups, especially those with plans to conduct an ICO. In November 2017, Estonian government clarified a business clause that helped prevent money laundering in order to ensure that ICOs in the country are regulated. And as if that were not enough, Estonia still has one of the most competitive fiscal policies in Eastern Europe, which favors investment in cryptocurrencies, not subject to VAT taxation. Also, ICOs are not subject to VAT or income tax, which makes Estonia one of the best places for cryptocurrencies industry as a whole (Schwarz, 2018).

France

French Minister of Finance, Bruno Le Maire, who proposed a discussion on bitcoin regulation at the G20 summit in 2018 (Reuters Staff, 2017), recently announced the creation of a working group on cryptocurrencies to be led by Jean-Pierre Landau (former deputy governor of France Central Bank - Banco da France), whose mission is proposing guidelines, monitor evolution of regulations around the world and suggest the best way to prevent the use of cryptocurrencies for the purpose of tax evasion, money laundering and financing of criminal activities and terrorism (Amsili, 2018).

Visibly opting for a proactive stance on blockchain technology regulation (Coindesk, 2017), French government has given its approval to new rules for negotiation of non-registered securities via blockchain, as well as for its financial regulators to draft legislation designed to attract business, through an "Initial Coin Offering" seal of approval, initial offers of cryptocurrencies (Murphy & Keohane, 2018).

Germany

Germany's finance minister has upgraded bitcoin to the equivalent category of "legal tender" when used as a means of payment.

Germany will not tax bitcoin users for using cryptocurrencies as a means of payment (BundesministeriumderFinanzen, 2018).

The guidance[52], published on 2/27/2018, separates Germany from the US, where the Internal Revenue Service treats bitcoin as property for tax purposes - meaning that if an American buys a cup of coffee with bitcoin, it is technically considered a sale of property and potentially subject to capital gains tax[53].

Instead, Germany will regard bitcoin as the equivalent of legal tender for tax purposes when used as a means of payment.

---

[52] In the decree of the sales tax application of October 1, 2010, BStBl I p. 846, most recently by BMF of February 7, 2018 - III C 3 - S 7433/15/10001 (2018/0108025), page BStBl I, in paragraph 4.8.3, after paragraph 3, the following new paragraph 3a is inserted: "Virtual currencies (cryptographic currencies, e.g. Bitcoin) are treated as a legal obligation, in so far as the so-called virtual currencies were accepted by the parties to the transaction as an alternative contractual and direct payment method and do not serve beyond their use as a means of payment (see ECJ). Judgment of October 22, 2015, C-264/14, Hedqvist, BStBl 2018 II p. Xxx).

[53] Higgins, Stan In: "US Lawmakers Seek Tax Exemption for Bitcoin Transactions Below $600", published at September 7, 2017, available at: https://www.coindesk.com/us-lawmakers-seek-tax-exemption-bitcoin-transactions-600/

The German Ministry of Finance has based his guidelines on a decision[54] of the Court of Justice of the European Union of 2015 on value added tax (VAT).

The court ruling sets a precedent for EU nations to tax bitcoin, while providing exemptions for certain types of transactions.

Notably, the new German document justified its tax decisions by considering crypto-currencies as a legal method of payment, stating:

> "Virtual currencies (encryption, for example, Bitcoin) become equivalent to legal means of payment, insofar as the so-called virtual currencies of persons involved in transaction as a

---

[54] Case C-264/14, REQUEST for a preliminary ruling under Article 267 TFEU, from the Högsta förvaltningsdomstolen (Supreme Administrative Court, Sweden), made by decision of 27 May 2014, received at the Court on 2 June 2014, in the proceedings, JUDGMENT OF THE COURT (Fifth Chamber), 22 October 2015, available in: http://curia.europa.eu/juris/document/document.jsf;jsessionid=9ea7d2dc30dd46d83cc58ff14e9e9407c3cc52516b72.e34KaxiLc3qMb40Rch0SaxyNb3j0?text=&docid=170305&pageIndex=0&doclang=EN&mode=1st&dir=&occ=first&part=1&cid=662540 , last access on 1/3/2018.

contractual alternative and means of payment were immediately accepted".

For tax purposes, this means that conversion of bitcoin into fiduciary currency or vice versa is "a taxable diverse benefit." When a buyer of goods pays with bitcoin, an EU VAT directive article will be applied to the price of bitcoin at the time of transaction, as documented by seller, according to the document.

However, according to EU decision, the conduct of converting a cryptocurrency to fiduciary currency or vice versa is classified as a "supply of services" and, therefore, the agent acting as an intermediary in this negotiation will not be taxed.

Payment rates sent to suppliers of digital portfolios or other services can also be taxed according to the document.

Other aspects of cryptocurrencies ecosystem will not be taxed. Miners who receive rewards collectively will not be taxed because their services are considered voluntary, according to the document.

Similarly, exchange traders who buy or sell bitcoin on their behalf as intermediaries will receive tax exemption, although a crypto currency trader that operates as a trading company will not receive such an exemption[55].

Gibraltar

Gibraltar legislature has approved a bill to update its financial services regulations, which lays the grounds for new legislation for the cryptocurrencies sector, financial services and online gambling (the main pillars of Gibraltar's economy) (Haig, 2017).

In the explanatory memorandum, the recently adopted law declares its intention *"to extend measures for protection of investors to licensed clients who carry out controlled activities other than investment services"[56]* (Government of Gibraltrar, 2017).

---

[55] To learn more about the tax treatment of buying and selling bitcoin and other virtual currencies, access: https://www.scribd.com/document/372651554/2018-02-27-Umsatzsteuerliche-Behandlung-Von-Bitcoin-Und-Anderen-Sog-Virtuellen-Waehrungen#from_embed

[56] Free translation of: "This Act amends the Financial Services (Investment and Fiduciary Services) Act to extend measures for the protection of investors to the customers of licensees carrying on controlled activities

Increasingly positioning itself as an attractive jurisdiction for cryptocurrencies and DLT companies, this last September, Gibraltar expressed its intention to develop a "complementary regulatory framework" for ICOs (Gibraltar Financial Services Commission, 2017).

India

Indian government, more specifically Arun Jaitley (India's Finance Minister), has taken a discouraging stance on cryptocurrencies in the country.

Jaitley referred to Bitcoin (Ministry of Finance of Government of India, 2017) as *"Ponzi Schemes"* (fraudulent scheme) in December 2017[57], and in January of this year several large banks in India

---

which are not investment services." (Government of Gibraltrar, 2017)

[57] "Government does not recognize encrypted coins as legal currency or currency and will take all measures to eliminate the use of said crypto assets in financing illegitimate activities or as part of payment system," Jaitley said. This is a translation of "Speaking about cryptocurrencies, Arun Jaitley, Finance Minister of India, just concluded the announcement of India's 2018 budget, where he said, and we quote," from the Indian site *ItsBlockchain* (Malviya, 2018).

limited or suspended accounts of cryptocurrencies brokerage houses, citing the risk of "illegitimate" transactions.

After criticism and Indian media interpreting his speech as an impending ban on cryptocurrencies in the country, Arun Jaitley gave an interview to an Indian newscast (DD News, 2018) and stated that there is no ban on cryptocurrencies in the country.

However, according to an article in the Indian Economic Times (Sharma, 2018), two Indian cryptocurrencies brokers BTCXIndia[58] and ETHEXIndia[59] have informed their clients via e-mail that they are stopping their trading activities, citing "stress" on their businesses caused by governmental organizations that discourage cryptocurrencies trading. BTCXIndia and ETHEXIndia websites showed a message to customers that deposits received after January 1 would be automatically sent back to the investor's bank account. BTCXIndia's clients were granted a term until March 4, 2018 to withdraw funds in Bitcoin (BTC), Ripple (XRP) or Rupee (INR), before an annual portfolio maintenance fee is applied. The interruption of trading at Ripple/INR was announced on the broker's website. There are no trading details for BTCXIndia listed on

---

[58] https://btcxindia.com/

[59] https://ethexindia.com/

CoinMarketCap[60]. ETHEXIndia customers told the newspaper quoted above that they had until February 28 to withdraw their Rupee or Ethereum (ETH) funds, and that the negotiations were halted on March 1, 2018. BTCXIndia[61], according to the same

---

[60]

https://coinmarketcap.com/exchanges/btcxindia/

[61] Here's the email message BTCXIndia has sent to its members: It's been 4 years since we opened BTCXIndia, and 2 years since we opened ETHEXIndia. We have served 35000+ customers during the years and have witnessed the BTC price go up 50x and the ETH price go up 100x. We have kept your crypto safe, and allowed you to trade against others on equal terms, in a safe environment, while adhering to KYC & AML and other tax compliance requirements.
As we heard in the budget speech, the Indian government is discouraging crypto currency trading. This has been clear also by government actions in the last year, and has put our business under a lot of stress and putting us in a position where we don't feel that we can continue our business in a professional manner any longer. Until new rules are in place for tokens on public blockchains, we are halting our trading (XRP/INR pair) platform and will focus 100% on our consultancy working with permissioned blockchains. All trading activity will be halted as of March 5th 2018. Please withdraw all assets from your account before then. Read more at: //economictimes.indiatimes.com/articleshow/6311 0237.cms?utm_source=contentofinterest&utm_mediu m=text&utm_campaign=cppst

article, on an email sent to clients, cites the budget speech of the Indian Finance Minister, and mentions it. And BTCIndia closes its e-mail expressing hope that the government will see the great benefits that Blockchain technologies can bring to India and may eventually promote progressive and clear regulation.

At present, what is perceived is a certain confusion among Indian authorities that, despite the intention to structure a regulatory framework on the subject (Gupta, 2018), since last year they are in a deadlock on which body will regulate cryptocurrencies (Choudhary, 2017).

This lack of definition of the Indian government, in turn, has already generated lawsuits. In April this year, Delhi Supreme Court issued a notice to Central Bank of India on receipt of a petition, addressed by Kali Digital Ecosystems[62], which seeks to safeguard the basic rights of cryptocurrencies entities to conduct any business. And in November last year, Indian Supreme Court had already asked the Indian government to respond to a petition requesting clarity on the matter (The Hindy, 2017), despite the government has been studying cryptocurrencies and proposing new regulations since April 2017 (Government of India, 2017).

---

[62] The Indian company that launches a call trading platform called CoinRecoil in August this year.

Israel

Interesting fact regarding the State of Israel is the recent decision of Israeli Supreme Court that issued an injunction prohibiting Leumi Bank from disrupting activities of the bank account "Bits of Gold", which is linked to negotiations in bitcoin. According to Israeli Supreme Court: "The damages that can be caused to the Bank ... are speculations at this moment" (Rubin, 2018).

In recent years, Bits of Gold, which acts as a brokerage firm and has the necessary approvals to operate, is fighting against Bank Leumi, which decided to close its bank account despite meticulous conduct of the company - just because the company is trading Bitcoin and digital coins. Since its establishment in 2014, Bits of Gold has an account with Bank Leumi. In 2015, the bank asked to stop all negotiations with Bitcoins at the bank, and then Bits of Gold decided to stand for the court for approval.

Japan

In the land of rising sun, Bitcoin was close to reaching mainstream, when in February 2014, Mt. Gox, (exchange established in Tokyo, and 70% of Bitcoin's global trade volume), closed its operations after its website was hacked, and about 850,000 bitcoins (in the average amount of US$ 450 million at that time) disappeared from their system. Mark Karpeles, Mt. Gox CEO, was arrested in Japan and charged with fraud and embezzlement (Wile, 2014). The real reason for the incident is still a mystery, and so the word "Bitcoin" in Japan has been associated with fraud, theft, and pyramid schemes (Ponzi scheme) for many years.

Following that incident, Bitflyer's cryptocurrency brokerage firm (a group headed by a Goldman Sachs ex-trader) began operations in the country, as well as *QUOINE*, another Singapore-based brokerage firm, also started operations in Japan. Little by little, these exchanges[63] have obtained a small number of customers, while some Japanese digital coins used on gaming sites have also emerged (Yagami, 2017).

However, 2017 was a watershed for cryptocurrencies in Japan. At the beginning of the year, China and South Korea repressed cryptocurrencies trade and closed the exchanges, as well as prohibited all ICOs[64], (*Initial Coin Offering* (Investopedia, 2018),

---

[63] Exchanges or crypto-currency brokers are companies that allow their customers to trade encrypted currencies (or digital currencies) for other assets, such as conventional fiduciary currencies (dollar, euro, etc.) or different digital currencies

[64] Ditto Note 18. 48 It's an Indian company that intends to launch a trading platform for

which in Portuguese can be translated by initial offer of coins and are nothing more than fund-raising activities related to cryptocurrencies (Meyer, 2017).

All of these events, combined with change in Payment Services Act (which is part of the Banking Act and has been changed to make cryptocurrencies a legal form of payment), have led to the sudden growth of cryptocurrency trades in Japan.

Here, it is important to note that the new Japanese law defined Bitcoin and other cryptocurrencies as a form of payment, not a legally recognized currency. Bitcoin will continue to be treated as an asset, unless there are future revisions or guidelines for Japanese tax legislation (BitFlyer, 2018).

"Official" approval from the Japanese government and restrictive policies in neighboring countries helped raise Bitcoin price, as well as boost digital currency turnover in Japan to 60% of Bitcoin's global volumes for a few days.

Another important milestone was the approval of the operation of 11 cryptocurrency brokers by Japan's financial authorities, FSA, in September 2017. At that time, 17 cryptocurrencies were admitted for trading in said brokerages, in addition to the main

---

crypto-coins called CoinRecoil in August this year

ones, such as Bitcoin, Ether, Ripple, Litecoin and Monacoin.

Finally, a group of Japanese brokers65, duly registered and licensed by Financial Services Agency (FSA), the country's financial regulatory agency, came together and laid out guidelines for self-regulation of cryptocurrency ecosystem in Japan. The launch of a self-regulatory body known as "Japanese Cryptocurrency Exchange Association" emerged to "restore confidence" in the industry after Coincheck's US$ 530 million stealing in January of this year (Yamaguchi, 2018).

Aiming at promoting a healthy trading environment, with development of standards for the entire industry, such as rules for customer protection and internal controls, seeking compliance of cryptocurrencies associated companies, the new body will also consider imposing penalties on members for activities that undermine public trust and confidence in the industry, and create and establish guidelines for initial currency offerings (ICOs) in Japan, working in conjunction with FSA.

---

[65] The 16 companies that make up the group are: Money Partners, QUOINE, BitFlyer, Bit Bank, SBI Virtual Currency, GMO Coin, Bit Trade, BTC Box, BitPoint Japan, Bitcoin DMM, Bit Argo Exchange Tokyo, Bitgate, BITOCEAN, Fiscal Currency Exchange , Xtheta and Tech BURO

The chairman of the entity will be Taizen Okuyama, chairman and CEO of Money Partners, and the new body will also provide guidance for other exchanges seeking registration but continue operating without an FSA license.

Mexico

Lawmakers in Mexico have reportedly advanced a bill that was drafted to regulate fintech, including cryptocurrencies, in the country.

The bill was approved by Mexican Legislature, and is currently awaiting the signature of Mexico's President, Enrique Pena Nieto, before it comes into force.

The latest Mexican legislative move aims at giving "green light" to the recently approved bill and ensure certainty of cryptocurrencies legal status, put cryptocurrency brokers operations under supervision of Central Bank of Mexico, as well as prevent the use of technology in illegal activities, such as money laundering.

However, the new law generally drawn, also foresees elaboration of a "secondary" law by other financial regulators, such as Mexican Securities Commission, Central Bank and Ministry of Finance in the next months (Reuters, 2018).

Nigeria

Nigeria was among the top countries that most used the word "bitcoin" for Internet search, according to Google Trends in 2017[66], alongside South Africa, Slovenia, the Netherlands and Austria.

However, according to a report by Quartz Africa (QuartzAfrica, 2018), Nigerian lawmakers see cryptocurrencies as a major Ponzi scheme and so Nigerian Senate has asked Central Bank (BCN) and other regulators to investigate the "proliferation of bitcoin" and seek to educate citizens about "the dangers of cryptocurrencies".

In this line, Nigeria Securities and Exchange Commission (SEC) warned[667] that potential investors should "exercise extreme caution" with advertisements about bitcoin and cryptocurrencies on

---

[66]

https://trends.google.com/trends/yis/2017/GLOBAL/

[67] "The Commission wishes to inform the public that none of the persons, companies or entities promoting cryptocurrencies has been recognized or authorized by it or other regulatory agencies in Nigeria to receive deposits from the public or to provide any investment or other financial services in or from Nigeria "

the radio and other communications channels (SECNigeria, 2017).

Russia

Government has issued a bill on initiative of the Ministry of Finance entitled "On digital financial assets"[68], which regulates creation, issuance, storage and circulation of cryptocurrencies and initial coin offerings (ICOs) in Russia. Let us see below its main points (Ministério das Finanças da Federação da Rússia, 2018).

The legal text brings the official definitions of cryptocurrency, tokens, smart contracts, exchanges of encryption and mining.

While cryptocurrency is defined as *"a type of digital financial asset created and accounted for in distributed record of digital transactions by participants of said record, according to the rules of maintenance of the digital transaction record [69]," a*

---

[68] Literal translation of: "О цифровых финансовых активах".

[69] Free translation of: "Криптовалюта – вид цифрового финансового актива, создаваемый и учитываемый в распределенном реестре цифровых транзакций участниками этого реестра в соответствии с правилами ведения реестра цифровых транзакций."

token is defined as "an asset type digital financial statement that is issued by a legal entity or an individual entrepreneur (hereinafter referred to as issuer) to attract funding and is recorded in the digital records registry." [70]

Mining, classified as a legally valid action, is considered *"an entrepreneurial activity designed to create a cryptocurrency and/or validation to receive compensation in the form of cryptocurrency."* Mining activities are subsequently described as *"legally valid" actions"*. [71]

In addition, the document clarifies that Russians have the right to exchange their cryptocurrencies for other digital assets and for the official currency of Russia, provided that through professionals licensed for the securities market. It is also provided in text of the law that holders of digital financial assets have the right to trade digital financial assets of one kind, for

---

[70] Free translation of: "Токен – вид цифрового финансового актива, который выпускается юридическим лицом или индивидуальным предпринимателем (далее – эмитент) с целью привлечения финансирования и учитывается в реестре цифровых записей."

[71] Free translation of: "Майнинг – предпринимательская деятельность, направленная на создание криптовалюты и/или валидацию с целью получения вознаграждения в виде криптовалюты."

89

other digital financial assets and/or to exchange digital financial assets for rubles, foreign currency and/or other assets only through the operator of digital financial assets exchange.[72]

Brokers must be "established in accordance with the laws of Russian Federation and perform the types of activities specified in Articles 3 to 5 of Federal Law No. 39-FZ of April 22, 1996 'On Securities Market'. Alternatively, they may also be "*legal entities that are trade organizers in accordance with the Federal Law of November 21, 2011 N° 325-FZ 'On Organized Trading.*" [73]

---

[72] Free translation of: "1. Владельцы цифровых финансовых активов вправе совершать сделки по обмену цифровых финансовых активов одного вида на цифровые финансовые активы другого вида и/или обмену цифровых финансовых активов на рубли, иностранную валюту и/или иное имущество только через оператора обмена цифровых финансовых активов. При этом указанные сделки, заключаемые с привлечением оператора обмена цифровых финансовых активов, являющегося организатором торговли в соответствии с Федеральным законом от 21 ноября 2011 г. № 325-ФЗ "Об организованных торгах", должны осуществляться в соответствии с Правилами организованных торгов цифровыми финансовыми активами, зарегистрированными в Центральном банке Российской Федерации."

[73] Free translation of: Оператор обмена цифровых финансовых активов – юридическое лицо, осуществляющее сделки по обмену цифровых

The document also imposes restrictions on portfolios, which are defined in Russian law as software and hardware tool that allows storing information about digital records and provide access. However, as a measure to prevent money laundering and terrorist financing, the Russian bill establishes that a portfolio should be made available by the digital financial asset exchange operator only after passing the procedures for identification of its owner, in accordance with the Federal Law of August 7, 2001. The document concludes that transactions related to negotiation of digital assets of persons that, according to the Federal Law of April 22, 1996 № 39-FZ, are not classified by Market Securities as qualifying investors may only occur through credit or debit of digital financial assets in a special account opened by the digital financial assets broker (which is owner of a digital portfolio used to store information on digital financial assets and can access

---

финансовых активов одного вида на цифровые финансовые активы другого вида и/или обмену цифровых финансовых активов на рубли или иностранную валюту. Операторами обмена цифровых финансовых активов могут быть только юридические лица, которые созданы в соответствии с законодательством Российской Федерации и осуществляют виды деятельности, указанные в статьях 3 – 5 Федерального закона от 22 апреля 1996 г. № 39-ФЗ «О рынке ценных бумаг», или юридические лица, являющиеся организаторами торговли в соответствии с Федеральным законом от 21 ноября 2011 г. № 325-ФЗ "Об организованных торгах".

the registry of digital transactions). The procedure for opening and maintaining said special accounts is established by the Russian Federation Central Bank.

Spain

While other countries seek to regulate more rigorously, Spain has decided to propose legislation in favor of cryptocurrencies.

Teodoro Garcia Egea, the lawmaker who is preparing the bill, believes it is in the European country's interest to welcome blockchain companies, as the new technology could boost innovation in finance, health and education, and hopes to have the legislation ready later this year. He also aims at making Spain a safe and friendly place to invest in cryptocurrencies, making it possible for investments in cryptocurrency below a certain amount not to be reported to Spanish authorities, while still providing an effective regulatory environment. "*We want to create the safest legal framework in Europe to invest in ICOs*" explained Garcia Egea (Duarte, 2018).

Parallel to this, People's Party plans to invite experts on blockchain technology to testify in parliament (James, 2018), which reinforces the perception that Spain intends to strongly join the race for innovation, following examples from Switzerland and the American States of Arizona, Tennessee and Wyoming .

South Korea

After Justice Minister Park Sang-ki said earlier this year that he planned to ban the trade of cryptocurrencies in its territory[74] (Kim & Kim, 2018), prompting more than 55,000 South Koreans to sign a petition calling for the end of repression to cryptocurrencies (Sil, 2018), the South Korean Financial Services Commission confirmed that some measures outlined by the agency were implemented on January 30, 2018 (CNBC, 2018). Among new rules is the closure of anonymous accounts in cryptocurrency brokers, so that banks can meet compliance[75] requirements and other legal obligations.

---

[74] This resulted in a sharp decline in Bitcoin's stock prices at local and foreign exchanges. Bitcoin's local price fell 21% in midday trade to 18.3 million won (US$ 17,064.53) after minister's comments. It still trades around a 30% premium compared to other countries. Bitcoin BTC = BTSP fell more than 10% in Luxembourg-based Bitstamp at US$ 13,199, after having fallen to less than US$ 13,120, the weakest since January 2 (Sil, 2018).

[75] Set of disciplines to enforce legal and regulatory norms, policies and guidelines established for business and activities of the institution or company, as well as to prevent, detect and treat any deviation or nonconformity that may occur. The term compliance comes from the verb to comply, which means to act

Shortly after South Korean government announced the new regulation, South Korea's biggest cryptocurrency brokerage firm, Bithumb, backed the idea. The exchange regards government regulation as a move that stabilizes, validates, and legitimizes the country's cryptocurrency market, a view shared by other actors in cryptocurrency market.

Sapien co-founder and CEO Ankit Bhatia says, "*I believe this is a movement that will help legitimizing cryptocurrencies. The expansion of this sector has been exponential, and these regulations are only growing pains*" (Drake, 2018).

In addition to ensuring investor protection, regulation of cryptocurrency market also aims to reduce the speculation that has attracted underage investors. South Korean reports show that thousands of college and high school students engage in encryption operations every day.

On March 23, 2018 (FSC - Financial Services Commission of South Korea, 2018), the South Korean Financial Services Commission published a new document in which South Korean authorities outlined a system similar to New York's "BitLicense" to be implemented by 2019, with a view to regulating cryptocurrencies market (BusinessKorea, 2018).

---

according to a rule, an internal statement, a command or a request (Wikipedia)

Switzerland

Switzerland has become one of the leading European centers for cryptocurrencies due to Crypto Valley Association, a cryptocurrency ecosystem and development of non-profit blockchain technology, launched in Zug, Switzerland, with government support and with the aim of *"supporting the development of technologies and business related to blockchain and cryptocurrencies "* (Crypto Valley Association, 2017).

The famous Swiss bank secrecy is under global attack due to anti-money laundering and tax evasion, but financial security remains on the agenda in Switzerland (The Economist, 2018).

Switzerland now intends to become a crypto-nation, in the words of Economy Minister Johann Schneider-Ammann at the First Crypto Finance Conference, an event held in the city of St. Moritz for worldwide investors (Schneider-Ammann, 2018).

In order to do so, Switzerland has favorable rules for cryptocurrencies and has encouraged the development of industries focused on products and services related to cryptocurrency ecosystem, such as the manufacture of hard disks (hardware) in which cryptographic keys are stored.

By 2016, Zug has become the first place in the world to accept bitcoin for some public services, and its residents can get a digital identity based on blockchain (The Economist, 2018).

United States

The laws enacted by legislature are the starting point for most regulatory regimes established by government and, in the United States, it is no different.

In the United States, most of regulations related to finance are under supervision of a regulatory agency, with SEC (agency responsible for capital market) by Federal Reserve, which has the power to create rules to implement general laws approved by the US Congress. These regulators are also responsible for records, licenses, inspections, certifications, and other supervisory activities in the United States. And when eventual civil or criminal laws are violated, the Department of Justice can also assist in law enforcement (Goodenough, Shrier, Hardjono, & Pentland, 2016, p.160).

As in the US, states and territories also have legislative power, we will analyze below important legislative initiatives of some American states.

New York and Bit license

Introduction

The term "BitLicense"[76] officially entered crypto-terminology lexicon when the New York State Department of Financial Services (NYDFS) issued rules for disciplining distributed electronic money, such as bitcoin.

The State of New York only allows trading of cryptocurrencies by brokerage firms that obtain a license called "Bit license" (which freely translated would be equivalent to "Credit License") issued by NYSDFS (New York State Department of Financial Services). As the industry has a very high entry level, there are 15 detailed regulations that require a certain amount of capital and financial reports quarterly. Well, that's why only three to four types of cryptocurrencies are authorized.

BitLicense

Since mid-2015, companies that trade Bitcoin and other cryptocurrencies have to obtain a license to operate in the State of New York. Before leaving the

---

76

http://www.dfs.ny.gov/legal/regulations/bitlice
nse reg framework.htm

97

position of chief of DFS77, New York Financial Services Department, he disclosed the rules that must be followed by bitcoin brokers to obtain the "Bitlicense", a "license" to operate in the State.

As head of DFS, Lawsky took on the role of regulating cryptocurrencies that were then used to buy drugs and other illegal activities on the Silk Road[78].

The 44-page document (Department Of Financial Services - New York State, 2015) states that "no person shall, without a license obtained from the superintendent, engage in any commercial activity in virtual currency." 79. In order to obtain a license, it is necessary to appoint a compliance officer to ensure that the company complies80 with the licensing rules and all other federal and state laws applicable to

---

[77] DFS, *"Department of Financial Services"*, has regulatory oversight over dozens of banks and insurers licensed in New York, including Goldman Sachs, MetLife and Barclays

[78] Idem Reference 13

[79] Literal translation of: "No person shall, without a license obtained from the superintendent as provided in this part, engage in any virtual currency business activity."

[80] Idem Reference 40

Bitcoin, such as money transfer regulations, laws anti-money laundering.

Demand of Bitlicense is quite controversial, generating criticism for those who see in their rules the increase of costs and restriction to innovation, besides placing already established institutions (financial institutions, for example) in a situation of advantage over new players (Whitehouse, 2015).

Wyoming

In order to maintain technological innovation in the state, Wyoming state lawmakers seek to make it the capital of US crypto-coins.

To do so, four bills could turn Wyoming into an ideal place for cryptocurrencies and Blockchain startups.

Among these projects, two of them (House Bill N°s. 0019 and 0070) have a significant impact on cryptocurrencies sector.

House Bill 0070[81] exempts exchanges of Cryptocurrencies from being legally considered to be stock-market or dealer brokers, as well as exempting the initial currencies offerings (ICOs) issued in an

---

[81] House Bill 0070, available in its entirety on: http://legisweb.state.wy.us/2018/introduced/hb0070.pdf. Last access on May 1st 2018

99

open blockchain to follow the securities laws of Wyoming, provided that token has not been traded as investment and can be exchanged for goods or services. *House Bill 0019*[82] seeks to exempt cryptocurrencies from state's money remittance laws, which proved problematic when cryptocurrency broker, Coinbase, abandoned the state (Zima, 2018). Both bills 0070 and 0019 have successfully passed the Commission vote and are ready for voting in the House of Representatives (Long C. , 2018).

Wyoming is one of the best places in the US to do business. Among low start-up costs, it has the country's most business-friendly tax system and legislators who are focused on supporting and fostering business growth and innovative technologies, such as cryptocurrencies and blockchain (Zima, 2018).

Internal Revenue Service (IRS)

Since 2014, the Internal Revenue Service (IRS) has considered bitcoin (and other cryptocurrencies) to be a kind of property for tax purposes, so any profit

---

[82] Bill of Rights, House of Bill 0019, of the State of Wyoming, available at: http://legisweb.state.wy.us/2018/Introduced/HBO 019.pdf. Last access on May 1st, 2018.

from trading cryptocurrencies can characterize capital gain and be subject to income tax[83].

In face of IRS positioning, two US Congressmen, Jared Polis and David Schweikert (who co-lead Caucus Blockchain in Congress), hope to alleviate some of the problems resulting from this decision with **Fiscal Equity in Cryptography**[84] Bill (Schweikert & Polis, 2017). If approved, the legal text would create a minimum exemption for payments made in cryptocurrencies below US$600, and transactions involving cryptocurrencies below the legal limit would not imply in capital gains for tax purposes (Higgins, 2017). As the text of the law says:

> "Gross revenue shall not include gain on sale or exchange of virtual currency for 5) other than cash or cash equivalents .... [if the amount of gain excluded from gross profit under

---

[83] Higgins, Stan In: "US Lawmakers Seek Tax Exemption for Bitcoin Transactions Below $600", published at September 7, 2017, available at: https://www.coindesk.com/us-lawmakers-seek-tax-exemption-bitcoin-transactions-600/

[84] To amend the Internal Revenue Code of 1986 to exclude from gross income de minimum gains from certain sales or exchanges of virtual currency, and for other purposes.

subsection (a) in relation to a sale or
exchange shall not exceed US$600.[85]

As for prospects of approval, it is worth considering
that this bill is in accordance with a movement of
American parliamentarians who seek to reform the
current US tax system.

Securities and Exchange Commission (SEC)

Securities and Exchange Commission (SEC), a
federal agency of the United States similar to the
Brazilian Securities Commission (CVM), which
holds primary responsibility for implementation of
federal securities laws and regulates the securities
industry has sought to apply securities laws for
everything, from exchanges of cryptocurrencies to
digital asset storage companies known as
cryptocurrencies portfolios.

---

[85] Free translation: "Gross income shall not
include gain from the sale or exchange of
virtual currency for other than cash or cash
equivalents . (...) The amount of gain excluded
from gross income under subsection (a) with
respect to a sale or exchange shall not exceed
$600."

US analysts have stated that SEC focus is not the bitcoin, but the new cryptocurrencies launched for fund-raising, the well-known ICOs, and they point to increased Commission efforts to crack down on initial offers of fraudulent tokens, which tend to allocate their potential profits to investors and have attracted billions of dollars globally. Coinbase, the main cryptocurrency broker in the US, declined to comment on SEC statement, and in February of this year, SEC chairman Jay Clayton said in a Senate Banking Committee hearing that he is open to exploring with Congress whether the increase of trading platforms regulation for cryptocurrencies is necessary or appropriate (Cheng, 2018).

What is a Bitcoin ETF?

An ETF is an investment vehicle that tracks the performance of a particular asset or group of assets. ETFs allow investors to diversify their investments without actually owning the assets tracked by an ETF. For those individuals looking to focus only on gains and losses, ETFs provide a simpler alternative to buying and selling individual assets. Further, because many traditional ETFs target larger baskets of names with something in common (a focus on sustainability, for instance, or stocks representing the video game industry and related businesses), they allow investors to easily diversify their holdings.

A bitcoin ETF is one that mimics the price of the most popular digital currency in the world. This allows investors to buy into the ETF without going through the complicated process of trading bitcoin itself. Moreover, because holders of the ETF won't be directly invested in bitcoin itself, they will not have to worry about the complex storage and security procedures required of cryptocurrency investors (Reiff, 2018).

If a bitcoin ETF merely mirrors the price of the cryptocurrency itself, why bother with the middle man? Why not just invest in bitcoin directly?

There are several reasons for this. First, as indicated above, investors don't have to bother with the security procedures associated with holding bitcoin and other cryptocurrencies. Further, there is no need to deal with cryptocurrency exchanges in the process; investors can just buy and sell the ETF through traditional exchanges and markets.

There is another crucial benefit to focusing on a bitcoin ETF rather than on bitcoin itself. Because the ETF is an investment vehicle, investors would be able to short sell shares of the ETF if they believe that the price of bitcoin will go down in the future. This is not something that can be done in the traditional cryptocurrency market.

Also, ETFs are much better understood across the investment world than cryptocurrencies, even as digital coins and tokens have become increasingly popular in recent years. An investor looking to get involved in the digital currency space but without the time necessary to learn about all of the ins and outs could focus on trading a vehicle he or she is likely to have a better understanding of already (Reiff, 2018).

The Road to Bitcoin ETF Approval

Firms looking to launch bitcoin ETFs have run into a difficult time with regulatory agencies so far. Cameron and Tyler Winklevoss, famous for their involvement in Facebook, Inc. (FB) and, more recently, for their Gemini digital currency exchange, had their petition to launch a bitcoin ETF called the Winklevoss Bitcoin Trust turned down by the SEC in 2017. The reason for the denial was that bitcoin is traded on exchanges which are largely unregulated, leaving it susceptible to fraud and manipulation. The Winklevoss brothers did not give up their efforts, however; on June 19, 2018, the U.S. Patent and Trademark Office awarded them a patent for a firm called Winklevoss IP LLP for exchange-traded products.

The Winklevosses are not the only cryptocurrency enthusiasts looking to be the first to successfully launch a bitcoin ETF. Cboe Global Markets, Inc. (CBOE), the exchange responsible for bringing about bitcoin futures, hopes that the SEC will permit digital currency-related ETFs, too. Cboe also acquired Bats Global Markets, Inc., the exchange on which the Winklevoss ETF would have been offered.

Why is the SEC not ready for a Bitcoin ETF yet?

While many in the crypto community seem confident that SEC approval for a Bitcoin ETF is just around the corner, on August 23, 2018 the SEC has rejected another Bitcoin ETF proposal — this time from ProShares. The moves follows the recent rejection of an application from The Winklevoss Bitcoin Trust. Better known as the "Winklevoss Bitcoin ETF" it was rejected for a second time by the SEC following a proposed rule change by BATS BZX Exchange, the exchange that had planned to list the exchange-traded fund.

But the SEC is not read for a Bitcoin ETF yet. The SEC thinks the bitcoin price is vulnerable to manipulation — and it is not buying into any arguments to the contrary.

Drilling down, the SEC's reasons for the rejection concern potential market manipulation, a lack of traditional means of detecting and deterring fraud and manipulation, and the lack of adequate surveillance-sharing agreements for the bitcoin market.

BZX had argued that the very nature of the bitcoin market made price manipulation "difficult and prohibitively costly" and produced several letters supporting this position. Not good enough said the SEC — citing a lack of data to support these claims — and concluding that "there is an insufficient basis in the record before it, to decide that the bitcoin spot markets are inherently resistant to manipulation."

Moreover, the SEC held that BZX had not been able to demonstrate that in the absence of traditional means of detecting and deterring market manipulation — through a surveillance-sharing agreement with a regulated bitcoin market of substantial size — that the exchange's own trade surveillance measures would suffice to prevent market manipulation (Lielacher, 2018).

Commodity Futures Trading Commission CFTC

CFTC is an independent US federal agency that regulates futures and commodities options and has among its objectives the protection of investors against manipulation, abusive trade practices and fraud (Investopedia, 2018).

Brian Quintenz, Commissioner of Commodity Futures Trading Commission, said in March that the definition of policies by applying the law is something that agencies in general need to avoid, and similar to the same line adopted by Japanese authorities, Quintenz said in an interview to CNBC network that an independent and private cryptocurrency body could help filling the gap between status quo and future government regulation, striving to establish and enforce the rules of the game (Quintenz, 2018).

American Senate

At a hearing called "Virtual Currencies: The Supervisory Role of the US Securities and Exchange Commission and Commodity Futures Trading Commission ", held in the US Senate on February 6, 2018, Jay Clayton, SEC president, and Christopher Giancarlo, CFTC president, made considerations about cryptocurrencies (The United States Senate Committee Hearing about Virtual Currencies, 2018). And in almost two hours of audience, we could extract some observations listed below.

According to SEC president, Bitcoin and Ether are not necessarily currencies (naming something of currency, or product based on currency, does not mean that it is not a securities title), just as most "utility tokens" are securities (calling a token of "utility token" or structuring it to provide some usefulness, does not prevent the token from being, in essence, a title.) Moreover, ICOS structure that involves the offer and sale of securities and directly implies in compliance with the requirements for registration of securities.

Clayton also says that brokerages where investors trade tokens are not really stock brokers because they have not registered with SEC, so many trading venues are even known as exchanges. Expressing concern, he said that investors trading on such trading platforms do not have market protections they would be entitled to, when trading through registered brokerages or alternative trading systems.

No ICO has been registered with SEC, and SEC has not approved any Exchange Traded Funds or other cryptocurrency derivative assets, and if anyone today says otherwise, investors should exercise caution.

Yet, ICOs have so far been vulnerable to digital hacking, with more than 10% of ICO gains (almost US$ 400 million) lost in such attacks.

It was also noted at that time, the need to implement anti-money laundering and KYC laws (know your client). And it was stated that the new Cyber Unit in the Execution Division will be more aggressive in enforcing actions against those who break the law. SEC Execution Division will continue to vigorously policing crypto assets and will recommend enforcement actions against those involved in cryptocurrencies actions in violation of federal securities laws.

Venezuela

Noting the success of Bitcoin and other cryptocurrencies, or by simple instinct of survival, the Venezuelan government launched the first national "cryptocurrency" [86].

It seems that Maduro sees in this technology a possible solution to the greatest political, social and economic crisis in the history of Venezuela.

According to the Venezuelan government, the national cryptocurrency, Petro is backed by crude oil. The country is a member of the Organization of Petroleum Exporting Countries (OPEC) but falling oil prices and crippling sanctions have seen the country experience one of the worst hyperinflation in recent years.

The Petro is for many people a lifesaver for a country in economic difficulties, the need to inject funds into the economy is serious and a token of its own could be a channel to achieve that. Many critics see Petro

---

[86] Cryptocurrencies are not issue by any government. The fluctuation of its price is only linked to demand and supply. Cryptocurrencies, which has a private nature, are issued and guaranteed by cryptographics algorithms (by mathematics and encryption). Cryptocurrencies are decentralized and they are executed via Blockchain (Revoredo, 2018).

as an attempt by the Venezuelan government to circumvent the sanctions that are being launched against it, especially between the EU and the United States.

Vietnam

Prime Minister Nguyen Xuan Phuc approved in August 2017 a plan to review and simplify relevant legal framework to cryptocurrencies in Vietnam. With this, it is expected that cryptocurrencies will soon be legally recognized in the country (VNA - Vietnam Business, 2017).

Phuc asked the Ministry of Justice to chair and coordinate with other relevant ministries and institutions (including the State Bank of Vietnam, Ministry of Information and Communications, Ministry of Public Security, Ministry of Industry and Commerce and Ministry of Finance), a thorough study of the current legislation in Vietnam, providing a comprehensive assessment and appropriate solutions to the Vietnamese regulatory framework.

The intention is that all normative documents on currencies will be concluded by the end of 2018, according to the first minister, with the compilation of a legal tax structure for cryptocurrencies by June 2019.

It is hoped that once the legal framework for crypto-coins is finalized, new possibilities will emerge in financial technology and online payments.

G20

The Presidents of Central Banks and Finance Ministers of France and Germany formally requested the Minister of Finance of Argentina to include cryptocurrencies regulations on the agenda of G20 meetings throughout 2018. Argentina currently holds the presidency of the G20 countries. In the letter, France and Germany want debates centered on monetary and political implications of digital currencies (Megaw, 2018).

This move to introduce cryptocurrencies agenda at G20 summit appears to be a strategy by France and Germany to position Europe as a region ready to embrace disruptive technologies. This is because, in official communiqué, the two countries recognized new opportunities in technologies underlying tokens, while mentioning substantial risks to investors in cryptography, and alerted to the need for appropriate measures to prevent that digital coins and Blockchain technology is used for financial crimes.

With the adoption of cryptocurrencies agenda by G20 summit, the subject gained evidence in a context of prohibition of the operation of cryptocurrency exchanges in China, and of implementation of new cryptocurrency regulation by several countries, such as South Korea, for example, which prohibits anonymous accounts at cryptocurrency brokers located in its territory.

The member countries attending the meeting held in Buenos Aires in Argentina, then, agreed that cryptocurrencies had to be studied, and more information would be needed before any regulation could be proposed.

At the end of the meeting held in March 2018, the month of July was set as deadline for recommendations on how to regularize cryptocurrencies throughout the world. Some conclusions can be drawn from the G20 Communique (Revoredo, 2018):

> 1) World economic leaders apparently prefer to call cryptocurrencies as "crypto assets," which implies seeing "cryptos" as assets rather than currency.

> 2) The G20 communiqué notably recognizes "technological innovation" underlying cryptocurrencies, with potential *"to improve efficiency and inclusiveness of financial system and economy more broadly."*

> 3) G20 members intend to discuss issues on the impact of

cryptocurrencies with regard to consumer and investor protection, tax evasion, market integrity, money laundering and terrorist financing, echoing concerns expressed by regulators around the world.

4) The rumors of repression to cryptocurrencies did not materialize.

It is a fact that, before any legal elaboration, mastery of cryptocurrencies essence and impacts in global financial system are necessary.

European Parliament

A document[87] requested by the European Parliament's Committee on Economic and Monetary Affairs was issued on July, 2018.

After an overview of the virtual currencies, this document points out the implications for financial market regulations and monetary policy (focusing on

---

[87] European Union, The European Parliament's Committee on Economic and Monetary Affairs, Policy Department for Economic, Scientific and Quality of Life Policies. In: Virtual Currencies: Monetary Dialogue, July 2018. The European Parliament, on June, 2018.

the possibility of central bank digital currencies). Whereas the content of this work is very relevant to the content of this book, the main priorities of the document are transcribed below.

One can distinguish between digital or virtual currencies on the one hand and cryptocurrencies on the other

While cryptocurrencies use cryptographic functions in the processes of e.g. authorizing or verifying transactions, digital currencies include all currencies that are implemented on computer systems (including, for example, in the form of a simple database). Cryptocurrencies can therefore be considered a special case of digital currencies. Characteristic features include the absence of a central counterparty, non-discriminatory public access, and security against fraudulent spending.

Currently, cryptocurrencies such as Bitcoin could not supplant traditional currencies to any significant degree

The available technology faces severe limitations regarding scalability. In particular, it would be prohibitively expensive to conduct even a moderate share of the transactions now handled via traditional currencies through cryptocurrencies.

Rather than as a medium of exchange, crypto and related assets are so far primarily used as a vehicle for financial speculation

Typically, cryptocurrencies are not based on sound underlying values, so it is hard to value them rationally. The associated large swings in value seem to attract speculators looking for outsized returns. Furthermore, it is hard to get a handle on the volatility of these assets in order to implement proper risk management (this fact supports high capital requirements as an appropriate regulatory response). The fact that they seem to be uncorrelated with traditional investments is therefore difficult to exploit through a hedging strategy.

Recently, a number of actors have tried to circumvent existing regulations on traditional financial products by the means of virtual assets (such as coins and tokens)

These include a considerable number of intransparent investment proposals that seem unsuitable for rational investors. Additionally, not all of the new assets fit neatly into traditional categories (e.g. are Bitcoins a currency, an investment vehicle, or, depending on the context, a bit of both?). Furthermore, certain trading practices that are prohibited on traditional exchanges as a threat to efficient market functioning are in use on crypto exchanges. Some regulatory refinements and clarifications could therefore be helpful.

The effects of a Central Bank Digital Currency (CBDC) can be disruptive

As long as cash, which provides valuable services such as anonymity of payments, is not abolished, a CBDC may not reduce the effective lower bound on interest rates very much. Monetary policy would still be constrained in that regard. Apart from that, the current fractional reserve banking system would be challenged at its core as soon as market participants increasingly held liquidity in the new digital currency accounts instead of bank deposits. To avoid recurrent instability of the banking system, commercial banks would need to come up with more reliable funding sources than deposits. As the fractional reserve character of the current banking system can be a major source of instability, such a disruptive change is not necessarily a bad development, but could finally pave the way for a more stable financial system.

CHAPTER 5|
REGULATION VS. CRYPTOCURRENCIES: IS IT POSSIBLE TO REGULATE?

Introduction

Are we going to use old rules, or do we need new rules to discipline cryptocurrencies? Is it really possible to implement regulation for technological innovations? Who will define it? What are the risks?

Not only legislators and regulators have many questions to answer, but we as a society need to work together to overcome these issues.

Therefore, some points that merit reflection will be placed on this topic in order to contribute to this debate between legislators, regulators and society, which is only in the beginning.

Cryptocurrencies and regulatory concerns

Media have constantly warned that cryptocurrencies and especially ICOs[88] are not regulated or are in a gray (undefined) legal zone. Nobody really knows what to do and which laws should be enforced. And, as regulatory agencies need to become active, they need to provide guidelines for challenges arising from cryptocurrencies. Understanding why these statements are frequently used by media is knowing some basic information (Bürgui, 2018) .... What is the purpose of regulation?

First, there is systemic stability that financial market regulation tries to maintain, which means that we are not just looking individually at this or that brokerage, this or that institution or industry, but we look at the system as a whole, and try to reduce and assess risks arising from existing connections in the global financial system.

---

[88] ICOs (or Initial Coin Offering) are a form of fundraising activity in which the new company issues new "currencies" in the form of a new cryptocurrency in exchange for a payment in Ether or Bitcoin. In comparison to IPOs, these are extremely easy to do and only this year have been raised more than US$ 6 billion (six billion dollars).

119

Protection of client and investor, especially for investors, is very important. In addition to the need to avoid abusive behavior in the market, i.e. prevent the use of inside information or fake information to ensure proper and efficient functioning of financial markets. And that is where regulation comes in.

In order to prevent abuses and protect consumers, a minimum of regulation is required to ensure that all market participants (brokerage firms, investors, for example) under the same type of risk are treated equally, without discrimination. And here, another important point must be considered: technological neutrality. Technology should not be regulated, but some regulation is essential to protect customers, investors and set the rules of the game in financial market. Regulate functions, not technologies.

Another point to consider is the fact that regulatory and legislative bodies are learning, as well as the entire cryptocurrency community, to deal with all these platforms, all of these networks. Here, you see how the extraterritorial nature of technology and lack of jurisdictional linkage associated with cryptocurrency (i.e. the ease of transferring cryptocurrencies abroad and the fact that they are intangible) makes it very difficult for any country to effectively regulate them without working with other governments. Not to mention that the regulator is always the last one to realize what is happening in the market, and the first one to be triggered when someone needs guidance.

In addition, it is worth noting that regulators and those who actually make laws have different roles in cryptocurrency ecosystem. When you talk about regulation and someone decides to settle in some sector, regulator should act. But it is not the regulator who legislates. Who creates the law are legislative organs, that is, the parliament, the National Congress and its Deputies and Senators. Regulators, in turn, only guide and enforce laws. But how should regulators guide and provide information on how to apply the law to this new phenomenon of Cryptocurrencies and ICOs?

There is always a relationship between innovation and risk. Regulators are usually averse to risk because they are what they seek to avoid, but it is important to emphasize that innovation must happen along with the regulator, seeking constructive solutions to new challenges that arise from the cryptocurrency world.

While some argue that it would be contradictory to think of cryptocurrency regulation, given the fact that they came precisely to counteract government interference in citizens' privacy and monetary policy [89], it is clear from the above that well-crafted

---

[89] Monetary policy is the performance of monetary authorities over the amount of currency in circulation, credit and interest rates controlling global liquidity of the economic system. (WIKEPEDIA, THE FREE ENCYCLOPEDIA, 2018)

regulation is crucial for the healthy development of cryptocurrencies ecosystem.

Consumers protection Vs Individual freedom

Regulators elsewhere say that it is part of their job to protect consumers from new and dubious cryptocurrencies, and therefore regulators are often quite cautious about warning consumers on the high-risk characteristics and price bubbles of virtual currencies.

It is worth reflecting, however, to what extent a protective stance is healthy, and in what sense should legislation on cryptocurrencies come: putting consumer protection always ahead of individual freedom of choice?

The answer, in this case, should oscillate, because innumerable factors such as educational level of the population to be reached by legislator, tradition that prevails in the country, among others, must be considered.

Here, as an example of a less taxing approach and more in favor of individual freedom, we can cite the position of Swiss regulators who, in face of the balance between consumer protection and individual freedom, adopt a stance that privileges individual citizens' freedom more (The Economist, 2018).

CHAPTER 6 | OUTCOME

A first point worth considering here, and as we have said in previous topics, is that we should not regulate technologies (Revoredo, 2018), but some regulation is essential to protect customers, investors and set the rules of the game in financial market.

Laws that require everyone to drive on the same side of the road can accelerate travel and improve traffic safety, standardized weights and measures make it easier and more efficient to manufacture products and services, and laws that prohibit Ponzi schemes[90] help reducing fraud and attracting more investors to the market (Goodenough, Shrier, Hardjono, & Pentland, 2016, p. 147).

---

[90] Ponzi Scheme is a sophisticated fraudulent pyramid scheme investment operation that involves paying abnormally high returns ("profits") to investors at the expense of the money paid by later investors instead of the revenue generated by any real business. The name of the scheme refers to the Italian-American financial criminal Charles Ponzi (or Carlo Ponzi).

In this sense, a regulation of cryptocurrencies could help maximizing benefits and minimizing damages, since it is not necessary to regulate the technology itself, which is quite debatable because of its dispersed and immaterial nature, but to regulate the environment around the cryptocurrencies, for example, rules for protecting the client and imposing penalties on those that undermine public trust in the industry, as well as stipulating guidelines for best practices by brokers, etc.

Of course, governments often use their power to protect existing interests, which may delay technological advancement, favoring both established actors and existing processes. There are, however, more flexible forms of regulation that favor good rules.

In regulatory systems, interventions and constraints in a given sector can be divided into two broad groups: restrictions and interventions that are applied before the exercise of an activity (*ex ante*), and the restrictions and ex post interventions that apply after the fact. The most extreme intervention is prohibition: total prohibition of an activity, followed by a civil or criminal penalty. Less rigorous approaches include regulation, qualification and supervision, often linked to demand for best practice, so that such ex ante approaches can especially discourage innovation (Goodenough, Shrier, Hardjono, & Pentland, 2016, pp. 156-170).

Thus, considering what is seen in this chapter, the best way forward is a more flexible ex ante regulation of cryptocurrency ecosystem, which ensures adoption of minimum standards of quality or conduct by cryptocurrency ecosystem actors, or a self-regulating body, with conduct regulations resulting from a joint effort between the sector's members and the country's regulatory agencies.

BIBLIOGRAPHY

Amsili, S. (January 15, 2018). *Le gouvernement nomme un <<Monsieur Bitcoin>>*. Access on March 20 2018, available in LesEchos: https://www.lescchos.fr/15/01/2018/lesechos. fr/0301151100963_le-gouvernement-nomme-un---monsieur-bitcoin-- .htm#formulaire_enrichi::bouton_linkedin_in scription_article

Anderson, N., & Farivar, C. (March 10 2013). *How the feds took down the Dread Pirate Roberts.* Access on January 15 2018, available in Ars Technica: http://arstechnica.com/tech-policy/2013/10/how-the-feds-took-down-the-dread-pirate-roberts/

Australian Government - AUSTRAC. (April 11 2018). *New Australian laws to regulate cryptocurrency providers.* Source: Australian Government   -   AUSTRAC   : http://www.austrac.gov.au/media/media-releases/new-australian-laws-regulate-cryptocurrency-providers

Bölle, M. d. (February 07 2018). O que é moeda? *O Estado de São Paulo.*

Bürgui, B. (January 18 2018). *Keynote speech: Crypto Currencies and Regulation: A Contradiction?* Source: Crypto Finance Conference: https://www.crypto-finance-conference.com/en/#pictures

BBC. (September 19 2017). *China orders Bitcoin exchanges in the capital city to close.* Sourcve: BBC - Business Section: http://www.bbc.com/news/business-41320568

Bech, M., & Garratt, R. (September 2017). *Central bank cryptocurrencies.* Source: BIS Quaterly Review: http://www.bis.org/publ/qtrpdf/r_qt1709f.pdf

bitFlyer. (2018). *The Virtual Currency Act explained.* Source: bitFlyer: https://bitflyer.com/en-eu/virtual-currency-act

Bölle, M. d., In: *O que é moeda? O Estado de São Paulo*, on February 7, 2018.

Bordo, M., & Levin, A. (May 2017). *NBER Working Papers, n° 23711, August.* Source: Central bank digital currency and the future of monetary policy: https://www.hoover.org/sites/default/files/bordo-levin_bullets_for_hoover_may2017.pdf

BundesministeriumderFinanzen. (February 27 2018). *Bundesministerium der Finanzen.* Acesso em 01 de março de 2018, available in Bundesministerium der Finanzen: http://www.bundesfinanzministerium.de/Cont ent/DE/Downloads/BMF_Schreiben/Steuerart en/Umsatzsteuer/Umsatzsteuer-Anwendungserlass/2018-02-27-umsatzsteuerliche-behandlung-von-bitcoin-und-anderen-sog-virtuellen-waehrungen.pdf;jsessionid=41D281B5241D4 7C388EF2F

Buntinx, J. (April 11 2018). *Australia Rolls Out New Cryptocurrency Regulation.* Source: NEWSBTC: https://www.newsbtc.com/2018/04/11/australi a-rolls-new-cryptocurrency-regulations/

BusinessKorea. (February 12 2018). *S. Korea Considers Introduction of an Approval System to Open Cryptocurrency Exchange.* Access on February 23 2018, available in BusinessKorea - Korea's Premium Business News Portal: http://www.businesskorea.co.kr/news/article View.html?idxno=20513

Calvo, G and C Végh (1992), *"Currency Substitution in Developing Countries: An Introduction"*, IMF Working Paper 92/40.

CBN, C. B. (February 28 2018). *Central Bank Of Nigeria.* Access on March 02 2018, available in Central Bank Of Nigeria: http://www.cbn.gov.ng/Out/2018/CCD/Press%20Release%20on%20Virtual%20Currencies.pdf

Cheng, E. (March 7 2018). *The SEC just made it clearer that securities laws apply to most cryptocurrencies and exchanges trading them.* Source: CNBC: https://www.cnbc.com/2018/03/07/the-sec-made-it-clearer-that-securities-laws-apply-to-cryptocurrencies.html

Choudhary, S. (July 22 2017). *Sebi, RBI engage in turf war over Bitcoin regulation.* Source: Business Standard: http://www.business-standard.com/article/economy-policy/sebi-rbi-engage-in-turf-war-over-bitcoin-regulation-117072101202_1.html

Christin, N. (July 31 2012). *Traveling the Silk Road: A measurement analysis of a large anonymous online marketplace.* Access on January 12 2018, available in Cornell University Library: https://arxiv.org/abs/1207.7139

CNBC. (January 2018). *Asia Top News and Analysis | South Korea.* Source: CNBC: https://www.cnbc.com/south-korea/

Coindesk. (December 18 2017). *France Wants G20 Natins to Discuss Bitcoin Regulation*. Access on February 5 2018, available in Coindesk: https://www.coindesk.com/france-wants-g20-nations-discuss-bitcoin-regulation/

CoinMarketCap. (March 1st 2018). *Cryptocurrency Market Capitalizations*. Access in March 2018, available in CoinMarketCap: https://coinmarketcap.com/all/views/all/

Crypto Valley Association. (2017). *Crypto Valley: About Us*. Source: Crypto Valley: https://cryptovalley.swiss/about-the-association/

CVM. (July 24 2012). *Deliberação CVM 680 de 2012*. Access in February 2018, available in CVM: http://www.cvm.gov.br/legislacao/deliberaco es/anexos/0600/deli680.doc

CVM. (Decmber 19 2017). *Oferta irregular – cotas de mineração de Bitcoin*. Access in February 2018, available in CVM - Comissão de Valores Mobiliários: http://www.cvm.gov.br/noticias/arquivos/201 7/20171219-2.html

DD News. (February 2018). *Bitcoin might be legal very soon in India - By Mr Arun Jaitley, Finance Minister of India*. Source: Youtube -

Ashish Mishra: https://twitter.com/zebpay/status/9593130272 57348096

De Filippi, P.. In: *What Blockchain Means for the Sharing Economy*, Harvard Business Review, 2017.

De Filippi, P., & Wright, A. (2018). *Blochchain and the law: The Rule of Code*. Londres: Cambridge Massachutts: Harvard University Press.

Department Of Financial Services - New York State. (2015). *TITLE 23. DEPARTMENT OF FINANCIAL SERVICES. PART 200. VIRTUAL CURRENCIES*. Access on January 20 2018, available in New York Codes, Rules and Regulations. Revised Virtual Currencies Regulation - Final Clean: https://www.dfs.ny.gov/legal/regulations/ado ptions/dfsp200t.pdf

Divya, J. (October 20 2017). *How the laws & regulation affecting blockchain technology can impact its adoption*. Source: BUSINESS INSIDER: http://www.businessinsider.com/blockchain-cryptocurrency-regulations-us-global-2017-10

DR. (December 18 2017). *Nationalbanken sammenligner bitcoin med tulipan-krakket i 1600-tallet.* Access on March 4 2018, available in DR: https://www.dr.dk/nyheder/penge/nationalban ken-sammenligner-bitcoin-med-tulipan-krakket-i-1600-tallet

Drake, D. (January 05 2018). *Will Regulation Legitimize Cryptocurrency Exchanges?* Access in February 2018, available in LDJCapital: http://www.ldjcapital.com/single-post/2018/01/05/Will-Regulation-Legitimize-Cryptocurrency-Exchanges

Duarte, E. (February 15 2018). *Spanish Party Weighs Tax Incentives to Lure Blockchain Firms.* Source: BLOOMBERG: https://www.bloomberg.com/news/articles/20 18-02-15/rajoy-s-party-weighs-tax-breaks-for-spanish-blockchain-companies

EUROPEAN UNION, The European Parliament's Committee on Economic and Monetary Affairs, Policy Department for Economic, Scientific and Quality of Life Policies . In: Virtual Currencies: Monetary Dialogue, July 2018. The European Parliament, on June, 2018.

Faife, C. (March 20 2018). *Canada Is Gearing Up to Regulate Cryptocurrency.* Source: MOTHERBOARD: https://motherboard.vice.com/en_us/article/d3 58zk/canada-is-gearing-up-to-regulate-cryptocurrency-parliament-hearing

Fatás, A., & Di Mauro, B. W. (May 14 2018). Cryptocurrencies´challenge to central banks. Access on August 31 2018, available in VOX CEPR Policy Portal: https://voxeu.org/article/cryptocurrencies-challenge-central-banks

Fernández-Villaverde, J and D Sanches (2016), "*Can Currency Competition Work?*", CEPR Discussion Paper 11095.

Fobe, N. J. (03/11 2016). *O Bitcoin como moeda paralela.* Acesso em fevereiro de 2018, available in Digital Law Library FGV: http://bibliotecadigital.fgv.br/dspace/bitstrea m/handle/10438/15986/2016.03.22_Dissertaç ão_Nicole_Fobe_Versão%20Protocolo.pdf?s equence=3&isAllowed=y

FSC - Financial Services Commission of South Korea. (March 23 2018). *Mandatory Disclosure of Corporate Governance to be Phased in from 2019.* Source: Financial Services Commission: http://www.fsc.go.kr/eng/new_press/releases.j

sp?menu=01&bbsid=BBS0048&selYear=201
8#34502

Galhau, F. V. (December 1st 2017). *Déclaration de François Villeroy de Galhau, gouverneur de la Banque de France Pékin, 1er décembre 2017 Bitcoin.* Source: BANQUE DE FRANCE - EUROSYSTÈME: https://www.banque-france.fr/sites/default/files/medias/documents/declaration_francois_villeroy_de_galhau_-_bitcoin_-_fr.pdf

GIBRALTAR FINANCIAL SERVICES COMMISSION. (September 22 2017). *Statement on Initial Coin Offerings.* Source: GFSC - GIBRALTAR FINANCIAL SERVICES COMMISSION: http://www.gfsc.gi/news/statement-on-initial-coin-offerings-250

Goodenough, O., Shrier, D., Hardjono, T., & Pentland, A. (2016). *Frontiers of Financial Technology. Policy & Fintech: How Regulators Think About Financial Innovation And How Financial Innovators Think about Regulation.* San Bernardino, CA: David Shrier and Alex Pentland.

GOOGLE. (December 28 2017). *Pesquisas do ano 2017.* Access on March 02 2018, available in Google Trends:

https://trends.google.com/trends/yis/2017/GL OBAL/

Government of Australia. (2017). *Banking innovation and FinTech - Australia as the innovation and FinTech nation.* Source: Budget 2017: http://www.budget.gov.au/2017-18/content/glossies/factsheets/html/FS_innov ation.htm

Government of Gibraltrar. (October 12 2017). *THIRD SUPPLEMENT TO THE GIBRALTAR B. 20/17 GAZETTE - BILL FOR AN ACT to amend the Financial Services (Investment and Fiduciary Services) Act.* Source: Gibraltar's Laws: http://www.gibraltarlaws.gov.gi/bills/bills201 7/2017B20.pdf

GOVERNMENT OF INDIA. (April 12 2017). *Government constitutes an Inter- Disciplinary Commitee chaired by Special Secretary (Economic Affairs) to examine the existing framework with regard to Virtual Currencies.* Source: Press Information Bureau - Government of India - Ministry of Finance: http://pib.nic.in/newsite/PrintRelease.aspx?rel id=160923

Greenberg, A. (November 6 2013). *'Silk Road 2.0' Launches, Promising A Resurrected Black*

Market For The Dark Web. Acesso em 20 de Janeiro de 2018, available in FORBES: https://www.forbes.com/sites/andygreenberg/ 2013/11/06/silk-road-2-0-launches-promising-a-resurrected-black-market-for-the-dark-web/#47c65c195714

Groendahl, B. (February 23 2018). *Austria Eyes Bitcoin Rules Based on Gold, Derivatives.* Access in February 2018, available in Bloomberg: https://www.bloomberg.com/news/articles/20 18-02-23/austria-seeks-bitcoin-rules-based-on-gold-derivatives-controls

Gupta, K. (February 03 2018). *Govt plans framework to regulate cryptocurrencies by fiscal year-end.* Source: LiveMint: http://www.livemint.com/Politics/58AmAqm 5fctlNVrQU06BFP/Govt-plans-framework-to-regulate-cryptocurrencies-by-fiscal.html?utm_content=buffer739bc&utm_ medium=social&utm_source=linkedin.com& utm_campaign=buffer

Haig, S. (December 14 2017). *Gibraltar Paves Way for Regulation of Crypto and DLT Companies.* Source: Bitcoin.com: https://news.bitcoin.com/gibraltar-paves-way-for-regulation-of-crypto-and-dlt-companies/

Hajdarbegovic, N. (March 19 2014). *Danish Central Bank Compares Bitcoins to 'Glass Beads'.* Access on December 20 2017, available in Coindesk: https://www.coindesk.com/danish-national-bank-compares-bitcoins-glass-beads/

Higgins, S. (September 7 2017). *US Lawmakers Seek Tax Exemption for Bitcoin Transactions Below $600.* Source: COINDESK: https://www.coindesk.com/us-lawmakers-seek-tax-exemption-bitcoin-transactions-600/

Hsu, S. (February 7 2018). *China Serious About Ending ICOs, Cryptocurrency Exchanges.* Source: FORBES: https://www.forbes.com/sites/sarahsu/2018/0 2/07/china-serious-about-ending-icos-cryptocurrency-exchanges/#6dc941e75675

Investopedia. (2018). *Commodity Futures Trading Commission - CFTC.* Source: Investopedia: https://www.investopedia.com/terms/c/cftc.as p

Investopedia. (2018). *Exchange-Traded Fund (ETF): Definition of Exchange-Traded Funf (ETF).* Source: Investopedia: https://www.investopedia.com/terms/e/etf.asp

Investopedia. (2018). *Initial Coin Offering (ICO).* Source: Investopedia:

https://www.investopedia.com/terms/i/initial-coin-offering-ico.asp

Itsynergis. (2017). *Legal Status of cryptocurrencies (digital-money) - Russian experience.* Access on February 2018, available in ItSynergis: http://itsynergis.ru/assets/docs/legal_status_cr yptocurrency_in_World.pdf

James, A. (February 18 2018). *Spain seeks to pass crypto-friendly legislation.* Source: Bitcoinist: http://bitcoinist.com/spain-seeks-pass-crypto-friendly-legislation/

Jia, C. (February 06 2018). *China to ban initial coin offerings.* Source: CHINA DAILY: http://usa.chinadaily.com.cn/a/201802/06/WS 5a78f237a3106e7dcc13af36.html

Kim, C., & Kim, D. (January 10 2018). *South Korea Plans To Ban Cryptocurrency Trading, Rattles Market.* Access on February 21 2018, available in REUTERS: https://www.reuters.com/article/us-southkorea-bitcoin/south-koreas-major-cryptocurreny-exchanges-raided-by-police-tax-authorities-idUSKBN1F002B

Lam, E. (December 15 2017). *What the World's Central Banks Are Saying About Bitcoin.* Source: BLOOMBERGY Technology: https://www.bloomberg.com/news/articles/20

17-11-26/what-the-world-s-central-banks-are-saying-about-cryptocurrencies

Lielacher, Alex. (August 23, 2018). *Getting real – Why SEC approval of a Bitcoin ETF remains a huge hurdle*. Source: Brave NewCoin: https://bravenewcoin.com/news/getting-real-why-sec-approval-of-a-bitcoin-etf-remains-a-huge-hurdle/

Lisk Academy. (2018). *Benefits of blockchain: what is decentralization*. Access on June 26, 2018, available in Lisk: https://lisk.io/academy/blockchain-basics/benefits-of-blockchain/what-is-decentralization

Loban, R. (January 2018). *Dealing with cryptocurrencies in Estonia - regulations and authorisation*. Source: HANDELSHAUS TALLINN - ESTONIA: https://hshaus.com/dealing-cryptocurrencies-estonia-regulations-authorisation/

Long, C. (February 14 2018). *Twitter: Today's update on the #Wyoming #blockchain #bills from the legislative session*. Source: Twitter: https://twitter.com/CaitlinLong_/status/963899114210476032

Long, G. (March 19 2018). *US bans trade in Venezuela's digital currency President:*

Nicolás Maduro launched the petro to skirt Washington's sanctions. Source: FINANCIAL TIMES: https://www.ft.com/content/2d2086ee-2ba0-11e8-9b4b-bc4b9f08f381

Malviya, H. (February 1 2018). *India is not Banning Cryptocurrencies - Stop the FUD.* Source: ItsBlockchain: https://itsblockchain.com/india-not-banning-cryptocurrencies-stop-fud/

Megaw, N. (February 09 2018). *Cryptocurrencies - France and Germany join calls for global bitcoin clampdown.* Access in February 2018, available in FINANCIAL TIMES: https://www.ft.com/content/03511abe-0d86-11e8-839d-41ca06376bf2

Menon, R. (January 11 2018). *Singapore sounds cautious note on cryptocurrencies.* Source: FINANCIAL TIMES: https://www.ft.com/content/2d433cda-f54e-11e7-8715-e94187b3017e

Meyer, D. (September 29 2017). *South Korea Follows China By Banning ICOs.* Source: FORTUNE: http://fortune.com/2017/09/29/south-korea-china-bitcoin-ethereum-icos-ban/

Ministry of Finance of Russian Federation. (January 2018). *Projeto de lei federal "Sobre ativos financeiros digitais".* Source: Ministério das Finanças -site Oficial da Federação Russa (Информация официального сайта Министерства финансов Российской): https://www.minfin.ru/ru/document/?id_4=12 1810

Ministry of Finance of Government of India. (December 29 2017). *Government Cautions People Against Risks in Investing in Virtual 'Currencies'; Says VCs are like Ponzi Schemes.* Source: Press Information Bureau: http://pib.nic.in/newsite/PrintRelease.aspx?rel id=174985

Morales, Y. (August 23 2017). *Criptomoedas: Carstens rechaza el bitcoin como moneda virtual; no tiene respaldo del banco central.* Source: EL ECONOMISTA: https://www.eleconomista.com.mx/economia/ Carstens-rechaza-el-bitcoin-como-moneda-virtual-no-tiene-respaldo-del-banco-central-20170823-0108.html

Murphy, H., & Keohane, D. (March 22 2018). *France plans rules to lure cryptocurrency business (Legislation would give stamp of approval to initial coin offerings).* Acesso em 3 de Abril de 2018, available in FINANCIAL TIMES:

https://www.ft.com/content/2e7b2778-2d22-
11e8-9b4b-bc4b9f08f381

News - Denmarks National Bank. (December 15
2017). *CENTRAL BANK DIGITAL
CURRENCY WOULD NOT RESULT IN
BETTER PAYMENT SOLUTIONS.* Access on
December 20 2017, available in Denmarks
NationalBank:
https://www.nationalbanken.dk/en/publicatio
ns/Documents/2017/12/News_Central%20ba
nk%20digital%20currency%20would%20not
%20result%20in%20better%20payment%20s
olutions.pdf

Norrie, J., & Moses, A. (June 12 2011). *Drugs
bought with virtual cash.* Acesso em 12 de
janeiro de 2018, available in The Sydney
Morning   Herald:
https://www.smh.com.au/technology/drugs-
bought-with-virtual-cash-20110611-
1fy0a.html

Perez, Y. B. (August 20 2015). *Nigeria's Central
Bank Calls for Bitcoin Regulation.* Access on
March 02 2018, available in CoinDesk:
https://www.coindesk.com/nigerias-central-
bank-calls-for-bitcoin-regulation/

Powell, J. H. (March 03 2017). *Speech: Innovation,
Technology, and the Payment System - At
Blockchain: The Future of Finance and*

Capital Markets. Source: THE FEDERAL
RESERVE:
https://www.federalreserve.gov/newsevents/s
peech/powell20170303a.htm

QUARTZAFRICA. (January 31 2018). *Nigeria's
lawmakers think bitcoin is on big financial
scam.* Access on March 02 2018, available in
QuartzAfrica:
https://qz.com/1194006/bitcoin-in-nigeria-
senate-warns-against-cryptocurrencies/

Quintenz, B. (March 7 2018). *CFTC Commissioner
Brian Quintenz talks about regulating
cryptocurrencies.* Source: CNBC:
https://www.cnbc.com/video/2018/03/07/repu
blican-cftc-commissioner-on-crypto-
regulation.html

RBI - Reserve Bank of India. (December 2013). *RBI
- Press Releases.* Source: Reserve Bank of
India - India's Central Bank:
https://www.rbi.org.in/scripts/BS_PressRelea
seDisplay.aspx?prid=30247

RBI - Reserve Bank of India. (December 5 2017).
Reserve Bank of India - Press Releases.
Source: Reserve Bank of India - India's
Central Bank:
https://rbi.org.in/scripts/BS_PressReleaseDisp
lay.aspx?prid=42462

Reiff, Nathan. (August 2, 2018). *Bitcoin ETFs Explained,* Source: Investopedia: https://www.investopedia.com/investing/bitco in-etfs-explained/

Reuters. (February 2018). *China prepares fresh ICO rules, eyes overseas plataforms: China Daily.* Source: REUTERS: https://www.reuters.com/article/us-china-bitcoin/china-prepares-fresh-ico-rules-eyes-overseas-platforms-china-daily-idUSKBN1FQ00U

Reuters. (March 1st 2018). *Mexico financial technology law passes final hurdle in Congress.* Source: REUTERS: https://www.reuters.com/article/us-mexico-fintech/mexico-financial-technology-law-passes-final-hurdle-in-congress-idUSKCN1GD6KX

Reuters. (March 1st 2018). *Singapore explores rules to protect investors in cryptocurrencies.* Source: REUTERS: https://www.reuters.com/article/us-singapore-cryptocurrency/singapore-explores-rules-to-protect-investors-in-cryptocurrencies-idUSKCN1GD3OL

Reuters Staff. (December 17 2017). *French finance minister calls for bitcoin regulation debate at G20.* Access on April 28 2018, available in

Reuters: https://www.reuters.com/article/uk-markets-bitcoin-g20/french-finance-minister-calls-for-bitcoin-regulation-debate-at-g20-idUSKBN1EB0SZ

Revoredo, T. (July 8, 2018). In: *Blockchain vs. DLTs: Brief comparative analysis of its underlying resources.* Access on August 31, 2018, available in Coinmonks: https://medium.com/coinmonks/blockchains-vs-dlts-8fe03df39737

Revoredo, T. (July 21, 2018). In: *Blockchain, We Trust: Meet the New Gatekeeper.* Access on August 31 2018,

Revoredo, T. In: *Criptomoedas: analise comparativa com moeda eletrônica e moeda estrangeira,* on August 27, 2018, available in Criptomoedas Fácil: https://www.criptomoedasfacil.com/criptomoedas-analise-comparativa-com-moeda-eletronica-e-moeda-estrangeira/

Revoredo, T. (October 27 2017). *Criptomoedas: cenário global e tendências.* Access in February 2018, available in JOTA: https://www.jota.info/opiniao-e-analise/artigos/criptomoedas-cenario-global-e-tendencias-27102017

Revoredo, T. (July 21, 2018). In: *Blockchain, We Trust: Meet the New Gatekeeper*. Access on August 31 2018, available in Medium: https://medium.com/@tatianarevoredo/in-in-blockchain-we-trust-meet-the-new-gatekeeper-733642da2463

Revoredo, T. (January 13 2018). *Reflexões sobre a regulação de novas tecnologias.* Source: JOTA: https://www.jota.info/opiniao-e-analise/artigos/reflexoes-sobre-regulacao-de-novas-tecnologias-13012018#sdendnote4anc

Revoredo, T. (November 6, 2017 - v1; last revised Apr 12, 2018 – this version – v2). *Legal "Status" of Cryptocurrencies in Brazil: Current regulatory regime and legal framework of cryptocurrencies – Brazilian experience.* Source: Medium: https://medium.com/@tatianarevoredo/legal-status-of-cryptocurrencies-in-brazil-273b712a0e50

Rosic, A. (2017). *What is a cryptocurrency exchange?* Source: Blockgeeks: https://blockgeeks.com/guides/best-cryptocurrency-exchanges/

Rubin, E. (February 26 2018). ‏העליון: לאומי חייב לאפשר מסחר בביטקוין בחשבון הבנק‎. Access in February 2018, available in The Marker:

https://www.themarker.com/markets/digital-coins/1.5850128

Scheer, S. (December 12 2017). *Bitcoin firms won't be included in Israel share indexes: regulator*. Access in February 2018, available in REUTERS: https://www.reuters.com/article/us-markets-bitcoin-israel/bitcoin-firms-wont-be-included-in-israel-share-indexes-regulator-idUSKBN1E61PN

Schiavon, G. (October 16 2017). *ENTENDA DE UMA VEZ POR TODAS O QUE É MOEDA CRIPTOGRAFADA*. Access in March 2018, available in Foxbit: https://blog.foxbit.com.br/entenda-de-uma-vez-por-todas-o-que-e-moeda-criptografada/

Schneider-Ammann, J. (January 2018). *Keynote Speech by Swiss Federal Councillor Johann Schneider-Ammann*. Source: Crypto Finance Conference: https://www.crypto-finance-conference.com/en

Schwarz, M. (April 03 2018). *Comment: Why cryptocurrencies are so popular in Estonia*. Source: INTERNATIONAL INVESTMENT: http://www.internationalinvestment.net/opinion/comment-cryptocurrencies-popular-estonia/

Schweikert, D., & Polis, J. (August 24 2017). *A Bill to amend the Internal Revenue Code of 1985 to exclude from gross income de minimus gains from certain sales or exchanges of virtual currency, and for the other purpose.* Source: CoinCenter: https://coincenter.org/pdf/CTFA.pdf

SECNigeria. (January 1st 2017). *Public Note on Investiments in Cryptocurrencies and other Virtual or Digital Currencies.* Access on March 02 2018, available in SEC NIGERIA: http://sec.gov.ng/public-notice-on-investments-in-cryptocurrencies-and-other-virtual-or-digital-currencies/

Sharma, D. (February 28 2018). *BTCXIndia, ETHEXIndia to halt cryptocurrency trading from March 5.* Source: The Economic Times: https://economictimes.indiatimes.com/wealth/personal-finance-news/btcxindia-ethexindia-to-halt-cryptocurrency-trading-from-march-5/articleshow/63110237.cms

Sheridan, E. (April 3 2018). *BOJ says: "Let's think about cryptocurrencies!".* Source: Forex Live: https://www.forexlive.com/cryptocurrency/!/boj-says-lets-think-about-cryptocurrencies-20180403

Sil, Y. (February 12 2018). *S. Korea Considers Introduction of an Approval System to Open Exchange.* Source: Business Korea: http://www.businesskorea.co.kr/news/article View.html?idxno=20513

Suberg, W. (February 23 2018). *Japan: Only 0,16% of 2017 Money Laundering Reports Came from Crypto Exchanges.* Access in February 2018, available in Cointelegraph, The future of money: https://cointelegraph.com/news/japan-only-016-of-2017-money-laundering-reports-came-from-crypto-exchanges

Takeo, Y. (April 2 2018). *Japan's Central Bank Wants You to Be Wary of Cryptocurrencies.* Source: BLOOMBERG - Technology: https://www.bloomberg.com/news/articles/2018-04-02/japan-s-central-bank-wants-you-to-be-wary-of-cryptocurrencies

The Central Council For Financial Services Information. (2018). *Let's talk about cryptocurrencies!* Source: NIPPON GINKO: https://www.shiruporuto.jp/public/document/container/kasotsuka/

The Economist. (February 24 2018). *Tales from the crypto-nation: A banking centre seeks to reinvent itself.* Source: The Economist - Finance and economics section:

https://www.economist.com/news/finance-
and-economics/21737255-switzerland-
embraces-digital-currencies-and-crypto-
entrepreneurs-banking-centre

THE G20 COMMUNIQUEÉ. (March 19-20 2018).
*Communiqué Annex Finance Ministers &
Central Bank Governors.* Source: The G20
Communiqué:
http://www.g20.utoronto.ca/2018/2018-03-
30-g20_finance_annex-en.pdf

The Hindu. (November 14 2017). *SC seeks govt's
response on plea to regulate Bitcoin.* Source:
THE   HINDU:
http://www.thehindu.com/news/national/sc-
seeks-govts-response-on-plea-to-regulate-
bitcoin/article20445197.ece

The Straits Times. (March 8 2018). *Japan punishes
crypto exchanges after hack.* Source: THE
STRAITS   TIMES:
https://www.straitstimes.com/business/compa
nies-markets/japan-punishes-crypto-
exchanges-after-hack

THE UNITED STATES OF AMERICA, United
States Senate Committee Hearing about
Virtual Currencies. (February 6 2018). *Full
Committee Hearing - Virtual Currencies: The
Oversight Role of hte U.S. Securities and
Exchange Commission and the U.S.*

Commodity Futures Trading Commission. Source: UNITED STATES COMMITTEE ON BANKING, HOUSING, AND URBAN AFFAIRS: https://www.banking.senate.gov/hearings/virt ual-currencies-the-oversight-role-of-the-us-securities-and-exchange-commission-and-the-us-commodity-futures-trading-commission

Ulrich, Fernando. In: "Discurso proferido em Brasília, na Audiência pública de 5/7/2017". Available at: https://www.youtube.com/watch?v=2GxaP koHNv4&feature=youtu.be. Last seen on October 6, 2017.

Vietnna.AT. (February 23 2018). *Finanzminister Löger will kryptowährunger strenger regeln.* Access in February 2018, available in VIENNA ONLINE: http://www.vienna.at/finanzminister-loeger-will-kryptowaehrungen-strenger-regeln/5680615

VNA - Vietnam Business. (August 25 2017). *Government considers recognising bitcoin in Vietnam.* Source: VNA - Vietnam Business: https://en.vietnamplus.vn/government-considers-recognising-bitcoin-in-vietnam/116916.vnp

Walton, J. B. (December 4 2014). *Cryptocurrency Public Policy Analysis.* Source: Virginia Commonwealth University: https://ssrn.com/abstract=2708302

Weiser, B. (May 29 2015). *Ross Ulbricht, Creator of Silk Road Website, Is Sentenced to Life in Prison.* Access on January 20 2018, available in THE NEW YORK TIMES: https://www.nytimes.com/2015/05/30/nyregio n/ross-ulbricht-creator-of-silk-road-website-is-sentenced-to-life-in-prison.html

Whitehouse, K. (3 de Junho de 2015). *'Bitlicense' rules regulating bitcoin released.* Access on January 20 2018, available in USA TODAY: https://www.usatoday.com/story/tech/2015/06 /03/bitcoin-bitlicense-lawsky-rules-final/28405317/

Wikipedia - A enciclopedia livre. (8 de Março de 2018). *Mainstream.* Source: WIKIPEDIA - A enciclopedia livre: https://pt.wikipedia.org/wiki/Mainstream

Wikipedia. (s.d.). *Compliance.* Access on January 20 2018, available in Wikipédia. A enciclopédia livre: https://pt.wikipedia.org/wiki/Compliance

Wikipedia. A enciclopedia livre. (2018). *Política Monetária.* Source: WIKIPEDIA. A

enciclopedia   livre.:
https://pt.wikipedia.org/wiki/Pol%C3%ADtic
a_monetária

Wile, R. (February 24 2014). *Bitcoin Exchange
MtGox Disapperars*. Source: BUSINESS
INSIDER:
http://www.businessinsider.com/reports-
mtgox-halts-all-trading-2014-2

Yagami, K. (November 2 2017). *Japan: A Forward
Thinking Bitcoin Nation*. Source: FORBES:
https://www.forbes.com/sites/outofasia/2017/
11/02/japan-a-forward-thinking-bitcoin-
nation/#60e01e3133a3

Yamaguchi, H. (April 24 2018). *Cryptocurrency
exchanges set up association for industry
rules*. Source: THE ASAHI SHIMBUN:
http://www.asahi.com/ajw/articles/AJ201804
240050.html

Zhao, W. (March 1st 2018). *Nigeria's Central Bank
Again Warns on Crypto Investiments*. Access
on March 02 2018, available in CoinDesk:
https://www.coindesk.com/nigerias-central-
bank-again-warns-on-crypto-investments/

Zima, E. (February 9 2018). *4 Wyoming BIlls Could
Boost Blockchain, Tech Growth*. Source: GT -
Government   Technology:
http://www.govtech.com/computing/4-

Wyoming-Bills-Could-Boost-Blockchain-
Tech-Growth.html

ABOUT THE AUTHORS

Tatiana Trícia de Paiva Revoredo. Founding Member of Oxford Blockchain Foundation. Blockchain Strategist by Saïd Business School, University of OXFORD. Member of Crypto Valley Association. Member of Government Blockchain Association. Patron Member at International Blockchain Real Estate Association. Liaison at European Law Observatory on New Technologies. Invited by the European Parliament to the Intercontinental Blockchain Conference. Participated in the largest worldwide events on Blockchain such as the 1st Annual Crypto Finance Conference in St. Moritz, Consensus in New York, Word Economic Forum in Davos, among others. Columnist at Blockmaster and Criptomoedas Fácil. Speaker and author of several articles on Blockchain and Cryptocurrencies. Court Legal Advisor at São Paulo Court of Justice. Specialized in Constitutional Law by LFG Business and in Digital Law by INSPER. Currently attending "Blockchain: Innovation and Business Application" at Sloan School of Management, Massachusetts Institute of Technology – MIT. Law graduate by Pontifícia Universidade Católica de São Paulo (PUC/SP).

Rodrigo Caldas de Carvalho Borges. President of the Startup and Entrepreneurship Commission of Brazilian Bar Association, Section Pinheiros and Founding Partner of CB – Carvalho Borges Law Firm. Founding

Member of Oxford Blockchain Foundation. Blockchain Strategist by Saïd Business School, University of OXFORD. Invited by the European Parliament for Intercontinental Conference on the use of Blockchain and regulation of ICOs. Participated in the largest world event on Blockchain, the Consensus in New York. Speaker and author of several articles on Blockchain, Master of Laws in Corporate Law from INSPER. Specialized in Digital Law by INSPER . Currently attending "Blockchain: Innovation and Business Application" at Sloan School of Management, Massachusetts Institute of Technology – MIT. Law graduate by Pontifícia Universidade Católica de São Paulo (PUC/SP).

www.ingramcontent.com/pod-product-compliance
Lightning Source LLC
Chambersburg PA
CBHW071305220526
45468CB00001B/281